D0314910

Haynes
Glovebox
CAR
BOOK

Steve Rendle

Haynes Publishing
Sparkford Nr Yeovil,
Somerset BA22 7JJ,
England

Haynes N. America, Inc.
861 Lawrence Drive,
Newbury Park, California
91320, USA

Editions Haynes S.A.
Tour Aurore - IBC,
18 Place des Reflets,
92975 PARIS LA
DEFENSE Cedex, France

Haynes Publishing
Nordiska AB
Box 1504, 751 45
UPPSALA, Sverige

© **Haynes Publishing 2001**

ISBN 1 85960 792 6

British Library Cataloguing in Publication Data
A catalogue record for this book is available from
the British Library

Printed by J. H. Haynes & Co. Ltd, Sparkford,
Nr Yeovil, Somerset BA22 7JJ, England

CONTENTS

MAKING
THE MOST OF
YOUR CAR

The average privately owned car has to be many things in the course of a year: commuter vehicle, school bus, shopping trolley, tow truck and holiday transport. This chapter looks at how your car can fulfil all these roles without costing you a fortune. Besides some of the more obvious ways of saving money on running costs, there are tips on how to avoid unwelcome bills in the first place and how to minimise the expense and inconvenience of a breakdown. There's also advice on security (yours and the car's), and on carrying children and unusual loads.

THINGS YOU SHOULD ALWAYS CARRY

It's a good idea to keep a few items in your boot to get you out of trouble if you're unfortunate to have a problem during a journey. It's worth noting that in some countries, it is compulsory to carry certain items, such as a warning triangle, first aid kit and spare light bulbs.

The basic tool kit supplied with your car won't allow you to do much more than change a wheel! It's a good idea to carry a few extra basic tools just in case - even if you can't fix a problem yourself, someone else might be able to help if you can supply a screwdriver.

European countries

Items indicated with ● are compulsory in most EC and other western European countries.

Documentation

In some countries it's compulsory to carry your vehicle documentation with you at all times (driving licence, certificate of insurance, vehicle registration document and vehicle test certificate), and you should do this in any case if you're travelling abroad. But remember not to leave them in the car.

MAKING THE MOST OF YOUR **CAR**

Emergency Kit and Spares

Here's a selection of items and spares which you might want to carry – the list could be endless, but it's a question of striking a balance between taking up space and having the necessary item to get you out of trouble.

▲ Fire Extinguisher ●

▲ Wheel brace with extending handle

▲ Can of water dispersant spray

▲ Warning triangle ●

▲ Roll of insulating tape

▲ Selection of hose clips

▲ First Aid Kit ●

▲ Selection of cable ties

▲ Windscreen de-icer spray (winter)

▲ Spare auxiliary drive belt

▲ Coil of stout wire

▲ Coolant hose repair bandage

▲ Spare fuses (10, 20 and 30 amp)

▲ Set of spare light bulbs ●

▲ Spark plug, properly cleaned and gapped (petrol engine cars)

▲ Ignition HT lead, to reach plug furthest from distributor coil

Tools

Here are some tools which won't take up much space, and will help to fix simple problems at the roadside. If you decide to carry out DIY maintenance, you'll need these tools anyway – refer to "Tools" for more information.

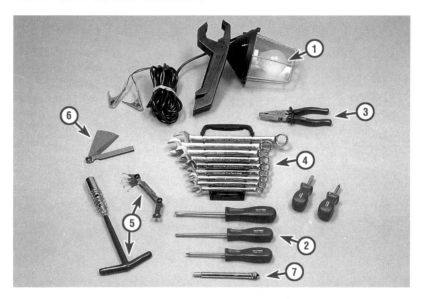

1. Extension light & lead, fitted with crocodile clips for battery or (preferably) cigarette lighter plug
2. Screwdrivers (1/4 in slot and crosshead, or combination)
3. Pliers
4. Combination spanners covering the range 10 mm to 19 mm, or elementary socket set
5. Spark plug spanner and gapping tool (petrol engines)
6. Metric feeler gauges
7. Tyre pressure gauge

CAR SECURITY

Car manufacturers are far more aware of car security these days, and many cars are supplied with etched window glass, immobilisers, alarms and protected in-car entertainment equipment as standard.

Apart from fitting security devices, there are several common-sense steps you can take to make life harder for would-be criminals. Some of the points might seem obvious, but the majority of cars are broken into or stolen in a very short space of time, with little force or effort required.

Etching

Have your car windows etched with the registration number or vehicle identification number (VIN).

This will help to trace your car if it's stolen and the thieves try to change its identity. Other glass components such as sunroofs and headlights can also be etched if desired. Many garages and glass specialists can provide this service.

Fit lockable wheelnuts or bolts which need a key

Especially if your car is fitted with expensive wheels. Alloy wheel are easy to sell, and are favourite targets for thieves.

1 Always lock your car

Even in the garage or driveway at home, or if you've just filled up with fuel and you're popping into the kiosk to pay. Many modern cars have anti-theft deadlocks – if your car has them, make sure you always activate them as a matter of course when locking your car. Don't forget to lock the fuel filler, and if the car is in the garage, lock the garage. If your car is stolen or broken into while it's unlocked, your insurance company may not pay for the loss or damage.

2 Put your aerial down when parking

Alternatively, you can have a telescopic aerial replaced with a less vulnerable flexible rubber one.

3 Protect in-car entertainment equipment

Most modern equipment is security-coded, and won't work if it's disconnected from the battery.

4 Fit an immobiliser

Electronic immobilisers will prevent the engine from being started. Mechanical devices, such as steering wheel and gear lever locks, can act as a visible deterrent.

5 Never leave valuable items on display

If you can't take it with you, lock it in the boot. Don't leave valuable items in the glovebox. Don't leave your vehicle documents in the car, as they could help a thief to sell it.

6 Close all the windows and the sunroof

If a window or sunroof is open, you're making the job of a professional thief much easier. A door can be opened much more quickly with the aid of an open window.

7 Park in a visible location

If possible, always try to park in an attended car park, and in a space where your car is highly visible. If you have to park at night, in a car park or at the roadside, try to pick a well-lit area (under a street light for instance).

8 Always remove the ignition key

Even in the garage or driveway at home.

9 Fit an alarm

The best alarms are expensive, but they will deter thieves. Many have built-in immobilisers; it's even possible to fit a tracking system which will allow the police to monitor the movement of a stolen car. If you have an alarm, make sure you switch it on even if you're only leaving the car for a few minutes.

10 Fit a Tracker

If you own a 'stealable' car like a BMW, a Mercedes, a sports car or a top end four wheel drive vehicle, it is worth thinking about a Tracker. It might seem an expensive option, but talk to your insurance company and see if you can do a deal. It might not stop your car from being stolen, but the thieves won't get very far.

When you're filling up, there are a few safety precautions which you must take by law . . .

NO SMOKING, and don't use a mobile phone whilst you're filling up

Keep an eye on how much fuel you've put in

Never fill the tank to the brim – if the automatic fuel cut-off stops the pump, the tank's full

FILLING UP

Although we all routinely fill our cars up with fuel without a great deal of concern, it's potentially a very dangerous job. When you fill up with petrol, vapour is released, which when mixed with the surrounding air, can form a highly explosive mixture. The biggest risks when filling up come from naked flames and sparks, and accidental spillage.

Top TEN filling-up tips

1 Stop the engine and switch off the ignition

2 If you're filling up with diesel, wear disposable gloves if they're provided

3 Remove the filler cap and put it somewhere safe

4 Make sure that the filler nozzle is engaged fully with the filler neck

5 Fill the tank slowly. Ease off on the nozzle trigger as the tank fills up

6 When you're removing the nozzle from the filler neck, make sure any drips of fuel go into the filler neck, not on the paintwork or the floor

7 Make sure you replace the nozzle in the pump correctly

8 Refit the filler cap, making sure it's secure

9 If you spill any fuel on the floor, sprinkle it with sand from the container provided near the pump

Leaded and lead replacement petrol
Leaded petrol is not readily available anywhere in the EC from January 2000. A substitute known as "lead replacement petrol" (LRP) is sold at the pumps. Anti-wear additives for use with unleaded petrol are also available.

Finally, don't forget to pay!

Don't be surprised if your fuel consumption figures vary quite a lot. If you take your car on a long trip travelling, the consumption is often different to when you're covering a similar overall mileage driving a few miles to and from work. You might even find that the consumption varies from season to season. If you find that your fuel consumption is higher than normal, and you can't find any other explanation, there may be a leak somewhere.
If you think there's a leak, don't drive the car (refer to "Leaks").

Why do I fill up so often?

Apart from an obvious leak, the biggest influence on fuel consumption is driving style – heavy acceleration, braking, and frequent gear-changing all use more fuel. Basically, the smoother the driving style, the more economical it will be. Poorly adjusted or faulty fuel system components can cause high consumption, and if you think there may be a problem, it's worth taking the car to a garage to have it checked.

To decide whether your car's fuel consumption is high, first of all, you need to have realistic expectations of what the consumption should be. Don't be surprised if your car doesn't meet the manufacturer's quoted fuel consumption figures – these figures are often recorded in controlled tests, simulating "normal" driving conditions.

Here's a quick guide to help you calculate fuel consumption. If you repeat this calculation for a few tankfuls of fuel, you'll get a more accurate idea of the overall consumption.

1. Fill your fuel tank, and zero the trip meter on the dashboard
2. Don't fill up again until your fuel gauge registers nearly empty
3. Read off the mileage on the trip meter before filling up
4. Make a note of exactly how much fuel you put in
5. You can now work out the fuel consumption as follows: – if you needed 10 gallons to fill up, and you had covered 420 miles since the last fill-up:

$$\text{Fuel consumption} = \frac{\text{Mileage covered} = 420}{\text{Amount of fuel} = 10} = 42 \text{ miles per gallon (mpg)}$$

Because fuel is sold in litres, you'll either have to convert the litres to gallons (divide by 4.55), or you can work out the consumption in miles per litre and then use this chart to convert to mpg.

Quick conversions

mpl	4	5	6	7	8	9	10	11	12	13
mpg	18	23	27	32	36	41	45	50	55	59

HOW TO SAVE MONEY

For most people, apart from looking after a family and running a home, owning a car is probably the biggest single source of expense!
If you work it out, the total cost of running a car for a year (fuel, insurance, servicing, road tax, depreciation, etc) can be frightening. There are lots of areas where you can easily make economies, or at least avoid spending money unnecessarily. Here are a few helpful hints.

The car itself

First, there's the choice between petrol and diesel engines. Diesel engines are generally more economical than petrol engines, and modern diesel engines are every bit as powerful as their petrol counterparts. Secondly, the smaller the car, the smaller the engine needs to be, and the more economical it's going to be – however, even if you're stuck with a seven-litre turbocharged monster, there are still ways to reduce running costs.

Insurance

It's always worth shopping around for quotes from different companies (but make sure the policies you're comparing are similar).

You can often reduce the cost by increasing your voluntary excess. This means that you will have to pay more if you make a claim, but your annual premium will be lower.

Savings can also be made by restricting the cover. It may not be worth insuring an older car with comprehensive cover, and inexperienced drivers on your policy will also push the cost up. Some insurance companies will also give a discount to members of motoring clubs, or if you have a security device fitted.

Depreciation

It's not until you decide to sell your car, or trade it in for a newer model, that you find out just how much money you've lost through depreciation since you bought it! The biggest amount of depreciation usually takes place in the first year of a car's life. If you buy a year-old car from a reputable dealer it will have a similar guarantee to a brand-new model, but someone else will have paid for that first-year depreciation.

Obviously, mileage has a big effect on depreciation, but there may not be much you can do to reduce the mileage you cover. Apart from mileage, the two main factors are the car's condition, and service history.

Driving style

The biggest influence on fuel consumption is driving style. Basically, the smoother the driving style, the more economical it will be. You'll also find that fuel consumption increases rapidly when the cruising speed goes up.

The law

Speeding tickets and parking fines can prove very costly. As far as driving and the law are concerned, if you break the law, you must expect to pay the penalty.

Other factors

Sometimes other factors increase fuel consumption, even though you haven't changed your driving style.

- Sitting in traffic jams
- Towing, or carrying a heavy load
- A roof-rack (increased wind resistance, even empty)
- Frequent short journeys (more fuel is used when the engine is cold)
- Long journeys in strong headwinds
- Long distances driving up or down steep hills
- Abnormally hot or cold weather

19

Do you need to use your car?

On short journeys (anything much under 10 minutes), the engine won't reach its normal working temperature, and fuel consumption (and engine wear) will be significantly higher than usual.

If you work close to your home, could you walk or cycle to work, or use public transport? You might even find it quicker than driving.

If you don't need a car to do your job, public transport could prove more convenient than driving, as well as cheaper, and far less stressful.

DIY maintenance

Have you considered carrying out DIY maintenance on your car? The cost of an hour's labour at a garage will pay for at least one tankful of fuel for most cars! Even if you only do the simpler jobs like changing the oil and filter, you can make a worthwhile saving. Details of the basics checks are given in "Simple checks and servicing", but if you're keen to learn more about how your car works, then a car maintenance course or an evening class at college will give you a more detailed picture

Top TEN money-saving tips

1 Don't buy a brand-new car; buy year-old or ex-demonstrator.

2 Check out insurance costs, servicing costs and fuel consumption before buying.

3 Shop around for insurance.

4 Drive gently. Your fuel bills will be lower, and you'll also avoid wear and tear.

5 STAGGER your journey times to avoid traffic jams – if stuck, switch off your engine.

6 Check tyre pressures regularly. Under-inflated tyres increase fuel consumption.

7 Avoid short journeys.

8 Consider buying supermarket fuel if it's significantly cheaper.

9 Think about doing at least some of your own maintenance.

10 Stay on the right side of the law!

MAKING THE MOST OF YOUR **CAR**

Fuel

For the majority of people, by far the biggest expense involved in running a car is the cost of fuel. If you've got into the habit of filling your car with fuel regularly, have you stopped to work out how much it's costing you over a year? This is worth thinking about when you're considering replacing your car

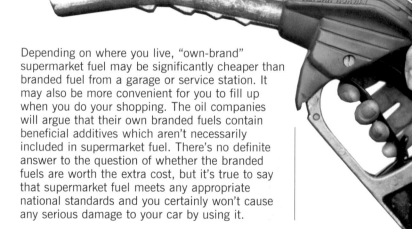

Are automatics thirstier?
Until a few years ago, cars with automatic transmission were slower and used more fuel than their manual transmission counterparts. Modern designs have all but eliminated these problems

21

Depending on where you live, "own-brand" supermarket fuel may be significantly cheaper than branded fuel from a garage or service station. It may also be more convenient for you to fill up when you do your shopping. The oil companies will argue that their own branded fuels contain beneficial additives which aren't necessarily included in supermarket fuel. There's no definite answer to the question of whether the branded fuels are worth the extra cost, but it's true to say that supermarket fuel meets any appropriate national standards and you certainly won't cause any serious damage to your car by using it.

Maintenance

A well-maintained car will always be more economical than a similar poorly-maintained example, and we're not just talking about engine maintenance. For instance, if the tyre pressures are too low, this will create more friction between the tyre and the road, and so fuel consumption will increase. (Don't, however, increase your tyre pressures above the manufacturer's recommendations in an attempt to save fuel!) Similarly, if the brakes are poorly maintained, they may drag, again creating more friction than necessary. So skimping on maintenance is going to cost you money in the long run.

TUNING UP

A tune-up means that the engine fuel and ignition system settings are checked to make sure that they're within the manufacturer's recommended limits. On older cars, a garage can check, and if necessary adjust, the engine idle speed, the fuel/air mixture and the ignition timing, but on most modern cars, these settings are controlled by the engine management system, and can't be adjusted (although they can still be checked if the right equipment is available).

When carrying out a tune-up, it's also a good idea to carry out all the checks which should be done on the engine when the car is serviced.
Provided your car is regularly serviced, tuning up isn't very often needed on a modern car, because there's not much to go wrong.
These are the main checks which are normally done:

- Check the engine oil level

- Check the coolant level

- Check the air filter

- Check the fuel filter (where applicable)

- Check the spark plugs (petrol engines)

- Check the battery

- Check the ignition and fuel system wiring and hoses

- A garage may be able to check the engine idle speed, the fuel mixture and the ignition timing, but on most modern engines, these settings are controlled by the engine management system, and can't be adjusted.

Do's and don't to keep your engine in tip-top condition

DO check the engine oil level every week, and before a long journey.

DO change the engine oil and filter at the intervals shown in your car's handbook, or more often if you can afford to.

DO check the coolant level and the drivebelt(s) regularly.

DO take the car out for a long run occasionally, if you normally only use it for short journeys.

DO stop immediately if the oil pressure warning light comes on when you're driving – it's not an oil level warning light, and you'll wreck the engine if you don't stop very quickly!

DON'T warm the engine up by leaving the car parked with the engine running – it's better just to start the engine and drive off straight away, even in winter.

DON'T warm the engine up by revving it more than normal.

DON'T rev the engine more than you need to until the temperature gauge has reached its normal position.

DON'T carry on driving the car if you know the engine is overheating.

Insurance

If you're fitting expensive accessories (in-car entertainment, or expensive alloy wheels), make sure that you tell your insurance company, otherwise the accessories might not be covered if they're stolen or damaged.

If you're planning to fit trim parts, such as sporty body kits, or spoilers, bear in mind that this could affect your car insurance policy – you'll normally have to pay an increased premium if the car bodywork has been modified, and if you don't declare the modifications to your insurance company, they may not pay up if you have to make a claim!

ACCESSORIES

Fitting accessories to your car enables you to tailor the car to your exact needs, and will give it a touch of individuality. There are a vast number of products available, and car accessories are a big business.

Where to buy accessories

Most car manufacturers have an accessories catalogue, and many contain everything you could ever possibly need!

Obviously, manufacturer's accessories will be designed specifically for your car - for example, tailor-made floor mats should fit perfectly and may incorporate your car's logo – however, this luxury usually comes at a price. You'll find that you can buy good-quality accessories from car accessory shops and motor factors far more cheaply than from an authorised dealer. Accessories sold by a reputable shop are usually of the same standard as the car manufacturer's own products – it's really a matter of personal choice.

Sometimes you can save money by buying second-hand accessories, but you need to be careful. It's a good idea to steer clear of second-hand electrical components, because it's going to be very difficult to tell whether or not they're in good condition, and if they aren't, they're likely to be difficult to repair. Beware of buying accessories from market stalls or car boot sales as there's little chance of getting your money back if they prove to be faulty or incomplete.

MAKING THE MOST OF YOUR **CAR**

Buying the right accessories

If you go to buy any accessory which is likely to be specific to your car (such as roof racks, towing hitches, etc), make sure that you have enough information to hand to ensure that you buy the correct components. You will normally need to provide the make, model, and the date of registration of your car, and you may need to provide the Vehicle Identification Number or Chassis Number – your car's handbook will show you where to look for these, and they can also be found on the registration document.

With some accessories, it's probably worth paying to have them professionally fitted. Accessories such as car phones and alarm systems can be complicated to fit, and the work may involve removing interior trim panels and tapping into the vehicle wiring. If you feel confident that you can tackle these sorts of jobs yourself, make sure that you follow the manufacturer's instructions. If you're having an accessory fitted professionally, and the work involves tampering with any part of the car, make sure that the work will be covered by a warranty.

If you're going to replace any of the car's standard components (such as the steering wheel or roadwheels), make sure you keep the old components (if they're in good condition), then you can refit them when you sell or trade-in the car. You can keep the accessories for your next car, or sell them separately.

Warranties
If your car is relatively new, you need to be careful that you don't invalidate the warranty by fitting non-approved accessories. This is particularly important with accessories such as alarm systems where fitting involves tampering with the car's wiring, or aftermarket sunroofs, where the body panels have to be drilled and cut (this may invalidate the manufacturer's corrosion warranty).

Car sickness

All you can do as a driver is try to drive smoothly, and provide a comfortable ride. Make sure that it isn't too stuffy inside the car (turn the heater down if necessary) and, if possible, leave a window (or the sunroof) open to allow fresh air into the car.

There are several forms of medication available to combat car sickness, but you should always read the instructions - if you're planning to give medication to a young child, it's vital to check that it's suitable. Don't exceed the recommended dosage.

CARRYING CHILDREN

Most parents strap their children into child car seats, confident that they've done everything possible to protect their loved-ones. However, many young children are travelling in car seats which have been badly fitted, or are being incorrectly used, making them potentially dangerous should they be involved in an accident.

Never allow children to travel in a car unrestrained – even for the shortest of journeys.

Never carry a child on an adult's lap or in an adult's arms – you may feel that your baby is safer in your arms, but this isn't the case.

Never rely solely on an adult seat belt to restrain a child – and always use an approved booster cushion to enable a seat belt to fit properly.

Always strap young children into a properly-designed child car seat.

Choosing a child car seat

Although age ranges are often given by the seat manufacturers, these are only a rough guide. It's the weight of the child which is important - a smaller-than-average baby can use a baby car seat for longer than a heavy baby of the same age. Never buy a second-hand child seat. Often, a second-hand seat is sold without instructions, and parts may be missing. This often leads to second-hand seats being incorrectly fitted or dangerous to use.

Your baby's first contact with the outside world is often on that first ride home from hospital, so make sure that you're prepared, and buy a baby seat before your baby is born.

These first car seats are light and easy to carry with a handle - this allows a sleeping baby to be carried from the car without waking.

All seats for babies up to around 9kg are rearward facing - this can improve safety, as the baby is supported across the back rather than purely by the harness, if the car suffers a frontal impact.

Forward facing seats, for when a child can sit unaided, use the car's seat belts to hold both the seat and child - make sure that this type of seat is fitted with a seat belt lock, so that the seat belt can't be pulled out of place or slackened.

Choose a seat which has an easily adjustable harness - this will ensure that the harness fits the child securely for each trip, and also makes getting a struggling child in and out easier.

Warning

27

NEVER fit a child seat to the front passenger seat of a car equipped with a passenger air bag - if an air bag is activated, it can cause serious injury.

Games and other amusements

Children need different amusements according to their ages and temperaments. Fighting with their siblings and kicking the back of the seat in front seem to be instinctive activities. Sleeping and reading are obviously the ideal pastimes from the parents' point of view because they are silent. However, children are unlikely to go to sleep on request and at any age reading may provoke car sickness. If this is the case, encourage games which involve concentrating on what is happening outside the car.

Pub cricket

The success of this game depends on the terrain – it's no good trying to play it on the motorway or in sparsely populated areas. Beware of foul play by the driver, who can influence the result by changing the route or driving a couple of times round the block.

Form two teams. One team takes the left-hand side of the road, the other the right. For each pub passed on your side, score one run for every foot or paw implied in the name, up to a maximum of 6 – so (for instance) 'King George' scores 2, 'Fox and Hounds' scores 6. Lose a wicket for each name with no feet or paws. The game stops when one team has lost ten wickets; the winning team is the one with the most runs at that point.

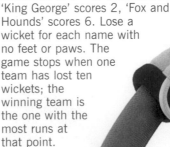

MAKING THE MOST OF YOUR CAR

Are we nearly there?
Older children can track the progress of the journey on a map, work out average speeds and likely time of arrival, help to calculate fuel consumption and estimate where the next fuel stop should be. Real clever-dicks can time intervals between mile or kilometre marker posts on motorways and pronounce on the accuracy of the speedometer.

Detective
Take it in turns to make up stories about the people you see in other vehicles. Where are they going? What will they do when they get there? What did you see which makes you think so?

Singing
Only if everybody agrees – a good diversion for those who are feeling sick, though. Singing the words of one song to the tune of another can be particularly amusing: for instance, the words of Abide With Me can be sung to the tune of Alexander's Ragtime Band.

Quiet please!
Offer a prize for the child who can keep quiet the longest – or for the spouse, come to that ...

Bonjour
If you're going abroad, practise some useful phrases for when you get there.

Keeping a child amused
Young children need to be kept amused when travelling in a car, so make sure they have a toy or two that they can play with without distracting the driver.

Remember
The load must be secured against sliding sideways, backwards and forwards.
Once you set off on your journey, stop after the first few miles to check that nothing's been moved or loosened by the movement and wind.

CARRYING HEAVY LOADS

Occasionally, you may want to use your car to carry a heavy or unusual load. Before you do, here are a few things to consider. Can you have the load delivered? Can you borrow or hire a pick-up or a van? If you have to use your car, can you make several trips?

Using a roof rack

If you're going to use a roof rack, make sure that it's correctly fitted to the car. Next, you need to make sure you load the roof rack sensibly. You'll usually find a maximum roof rack load specified in your car's handbook – don't exceed it!

Even an empty roof rack can cause about a 10% increase in fuel consumption, and if you load up a roof rack without thinking, it can be even worse – ideally you're aiming for the minimum possible amount of wind resistance.

Before you put anything on the roof rack, spread a large sheet of plastic or a tarpaulin over the rack (make sure that it's big enough to wrap completely around the load).

Load the roof rack with the largest items at the rear, and the smallest items at the front.

Wrap the plastic or tarpaulin around the load, trying to arrange the overlap so that the wind won't catch it. Secure it with suitable tie-downs (use the self-locking type with a metal buckle), rope, or elastic cords – an "octopus"-style load bungee is ideal.

Make sure the roof rack and load are secure – give them a good pull in all directions before setting off, and if necessary, add additional securing straps.

Roof racks

Some roof racks claim to be "universal", while others are tailor-made for a particular model of car. On some cars, you may have no option but to use the car manufacturer's own roof rails or rack. Many manufacturers produce complete luggage carrying systems, with roof rails, and compatible luggage trays, cycle carriers, etc. Often, you can buy a basic set of roof rails, or a rack, with a separate mounting adapter kit to fit your car – this means you'll still be able to use the unit if you change your car, you just buy the appropriate adapter kit.

Rails and racks
Rails fit into tracks running the length of the roof. You can then buy adjustable racks that fix easily onto the rails.

Top box
These come in various sizes. Their aerodynamic shape helps to keep down wind resistance, and most can be locked.

Ski box
This type of top box is handy for carrying equipment for any sport that has awkwardly shaped accessories.

Carrying bikes
Putting bikes on the car roof is another alternative to carrying them on the rear-mounted carrier.

CARRYING LONG LOADS

If you have to carry an unusually long load, the best place to put it is on a roof rack – make sure the load is properly secured, and can't slide forwards or backwards.

If you can't put the load on a roof rack, fold down the rear seats (if possible), and slide the load in beside the front passenger seat – you may be able to fold or recline the seat to give more room. Make sure the load is secure, and doesn't interfere with the driver's controls. If you can't fully close the boot lid or tailgate, make sure it's held securely with rope or a tie-down, and make sure that the number plate and rear lights are still visible.

On cars with a sunroof it's sometimes possible to carry ladders or planks poking

out through the opened roof.

If you use this method, make sure that the load is secured against sliding into the driver on bends.

If you can't load the car through the boot, slide the load through a back window, and rest it beside the front passenger seat. NEVER slide a load through a front window, with the load facing forwards.

SAFETY WITH LOADS

Before you start loading the car, consider the safety (and legal) implications.

Load the car sensibly – how many cars have you seen driving back from the ferry port full of "duty-free", with the rear suspension on the bump stops and the headlights pointing at the sky? If the suspension can't do its job it's dangerous, and it's also likely to cause damage to the car. Make sure your headlight beams are adjusted to compensate for any load.

Never exceed the "maximum gross vehicle weight" - this will be given in your car's handbook.

Make sure that the load doesn't affect your visibility – if you can't see through the back window, make sure that your door mirrors are adjusted so you can still see behind you. Never allow anything to hang down over the windscreen.

Increase your tyre pressures when carrying a heavy load – consult your car's handbook for details. You may need to inflate your tyres to the "full-load" pressures.

Make sure that your car's rear number plate and lights are visible – it's against the law to drive with a number plate or light obscured, and it's dangerous.

Cycle carriers
There's a wide range of specialist cycle carriers available. Which system suits you best is very much down to personal choice – but if you opt for a cycle carrier which fits on the rear of the car, you'll still be able to use a roof rack.
Something to bear in mind if you use a rear-mounted carrier is that you must still be able to read the car's rear number plate and see all the rear lights. You'll probably have to buy an additional rear number plate, and you may even have to fit a set of lights (make sure that they're correctly wired).

33

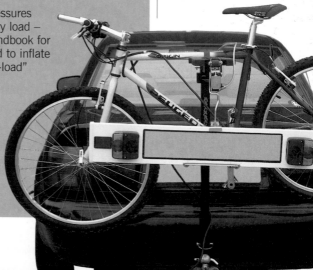

TOWING

If you're towing for the first time, there are a few points to bear in mind. First, make sure you have a tow bar which is up to the job! If you can afford it, it's worth paying for a professional installation. Make sure you're familiar with any laws which apply, especially if you're travelling abroad. In particular, make sure you know the speed limits. In some countries you need a separate warning light fitted in the car to show that the trailer/caravan direction indicator lights are working.

Before starting a journey

Make sure your car can cope with the load – are the engine, brakes, tyres and suspension up to the job?

Don't exceed the maximum trailer or tow bar weights for the car – check your car's handbook for details.

Make sure you can see behind the trailer/caravan – using the car's mirrors. Extending side mirrors can be fitted to most cars.

Make sure the tyre pressures are correct – unless you're towing a light, unladen trailer, the car tyres should be inflated to the "full load" pressures (check your car's handbook). Check the

trailer/caravan tyre pressures are correct too. Make sure the headlights are set correctly – check the aim with the trailer/caravan attached, and have it adjusted if necessary. Many cars have an adjuster on the dashboard.

Make sure the trailer/caravan lights work correctly – the extra load on the flasher circuit may cause the indicators to flash too slowly, so you may need a "heavy duty" flasher unit.

Make sure that the trailer/caravan is correctly loaded – refer to the manufacturer's recommendations. As a general rule, distribute the weight with the heaviest items as near as possible to the trailer/caravan axle. Secure all heavy items so they can't move. Car manufacturers usually specify an optimum noseweight for a trailer/caravan when loaded. If necessary, move the load to get as close as possible to the recommended noseweight. Don't exceed the recommended noseweight.

Engine – Don't put unnecessary strain on the engine by trying to tow a very heavy load. The extra load on an engine when towing may mean that the cooling system is no longer adequate – you may be able to have modified cooling system components (a larger radiator, etc) fitted to cope with this if you tow regularly.

Suspension – Towing puts extra strain on a car's suspension components, and can affect the handling of a car. Heavy duty rear suspension components are available for most cars to cope with towing.

Driving tips

Avoid driving with an unladen car and a loaded trailer/caravan – the uneven weight distribution will make the car unstable.

Always drive at a safe speed – always reduce speed in bad weather and high winds – especially when driving downhill. If there are any signs of "snaking", slow down immediately but gently – never try accelerating, and don't brake hard either.

Always brake in good time – if the trailer/caravan has brakes, apply the brakes gently at first, then firmly. This will prevent the trailer/caravan wheels from locking. If the car has a manual transmission, change before going down a steep hill (the engine will act as a brake), and on cars with automatic transmission, select "2" or "1" in the case of very steep hills.

Don't use a lower gear unnecessarily – stay in as high a gear as possible, to keep the engine revs low, but don't let the engine labour. This helps to avoid engine overheating.

Make sure you know how to reverse – this can be tricky if you've never done it before.

STRAIGHT-LINE REVERSING

Reversing a caravan is another skill that might seem impossible to master – but, once again, it can be perfectly straightforward. It's easy to reverse a car in a straight line but with a trailer behind you there is a new set of rules to use. Once you understand these, you should have no problems at all.

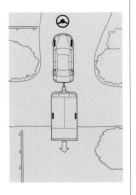

Start out straight

1 Straight-line reversing onto a pitch is a vital skill, and one that you can master easily if you adopt the right techniques from the start. It's a good idea for a passenger to step out of the car and stand in their communicating position to the rear and side of the caravan. Then look for objects such as low posts, walls, children's bicycles and so on, which may be in your way and which you cannot see. Start reversing as you would normally, with your steering wheel straight.

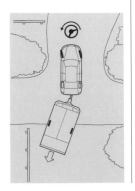

Veering one way...

2 Check each extension mirror in turn. If you see the back end of the caravan appearing in one of them, this means that the caravan is starting to veer, and you need to correct it to stop it going further in that direction. Here, the caravan has appeared in the left-hand extension mirror. To straighten up, steer smoothly towards the mirror in which the caravan appears (left), very slightly, and it will disappear.

The Theory

It may seem a difficult concept to grasp at first, but instead of being able to turn your car steering in the direction that you want your caravan to go, you must turn it in the OPPOSITE direction. Because this is completely different to the way in which you manoeuvre a car when there is no caravan on the back, it will take you some time and a little practice to get the angle of manoeuvring correct. This is especially critical when it comes to reversing around corners (see pages 39 to 41). When reversing in a straight line, the easiest way to remember what to do is to tell yourself to steer towards the towing mirror in which the caravan appears.

...and then the other

3 Now start checking each mirror in turn once again and you will probably find that, however carefully you undertook your correction, the caravan has appeared in the other mirror. Here the caravan is in the right-hand mirror and so the steering wheel is being turned very slightly to the right to correct the movement. Remember to keep your steering movements smooth and gentle.

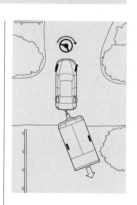

Back on the straight

4 If you've corrected properly, you should now be reversing in a straight line. Once you have practised reversing in this way a few times you will know when and how to correct the slightest movement. If you need to build up your confidence, go to a large open area such as a supermarket car park or old airfield, and practise. Remember, take your time, look carefully in the mirrors and make your corrections smoothly, in plenty of time.

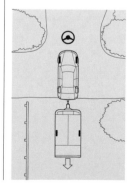

Effective Correction

If you steer too sharply in order to correct the movement of the caravan, it will simply disappear out of one mirror and appear immediately in the other. This will leave you constantly correcting and your car waggling from side to side – hardly a smooth progression.

If you do oversteer or don't correct in time, stop and pull forwards a couple of metres to straighten out the outfit, and then start again.

Successful Straight-Line Reversing

- **Remember**, it's just a case of 'look and steer to correct' – there is no secret formula

- **Correct little** but often to keep a smooth rearward progression

- **Don't** be put off by your new neighbours watching you reversing onto your pitch – they're probably not giving you marks out of 10!

- A helper **standing** to the rear of the caravan but in view of your mirrors will be able to let you know about obstacles that you can't see yourself

- **Practise** wherever and whenever you can – this will help you gain in skill and confidence

REVERSING ROUND CORNERS

Once you have mastered straight-line reversing, you will have enough skill and feel for your caravan to enable you to reverse around corners without too much trouble. You will probably not have to do this type of reversing very often, but you never know when a good working knowledge of the procedure will come in useful.

39

Successful Reversing Round Corners

- Start off correctly: if you are turning round a left-hand corner, steer to the right first. If you are reversing round a right-hand corner, steer left first

- Once the caravan has started to turn, reverse the direction of the steering wheel to help get the caravan round the corner smoothly

- If the caravan is taking the corner too sharply, steer back, very slightly, towards the original direction

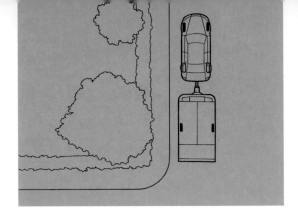

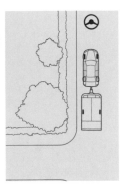

Take it slowly

1 As with reversing in a straight line, you may need a helper to keep an eye on things behind as you go back. Don't go any faster than walking pace – so that you can anticipate and correct any mistakes early on. And don't expect to be able to turn the wheel and watch the caravan go round the corner in one smooth movement. To reverse round a left-hand corner (shown here), keep your car and caravan aligned as you start to go back straight, and then turn your steering wheel to the right.

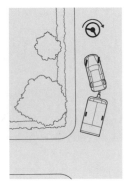

Starting to turn

2 As you reverse and slowly turn the steering wheel to the right, the car's wheels also move to the right and the car pushes the caravan round to the left, as it starts to take the corner. Keep looking ahead and in your mirrors as the car starts to swing out, as you would when reversing normally, and be prepared to stop at any time in order to let any other traffic pass safely.

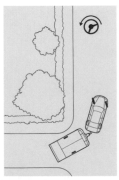

Going round

3 Once the caravan has started to turn round the corner, change the direction of the steering wheel and turn it to the left, too. This will keep the caravan going round the corner in a smooth arc.

MAKING THE MOST OF YOUR CAR

Going in too tight

4 If the caravan appears to be cornering too sharply, correct the movement by steering back to the right a little, carefully. Don't make a large steering wheel turn at this point to try and compensate – this will probably only make things worse.

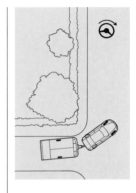

41

Avoiding a jackknife

5 If it is too late, and the caravan has already cornered too sharply, then stop. If you don't, the caravan may 'jackknife' and the front edge of the caravan could come into contact with the back of the car, causing damage. If you are in a potential jackknife situation, stop and pull forwards a few metres until the outfit is straight. Then try again.

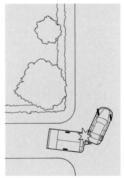

To reverse around a right-hand corner, simply follow the opposite procedure. You will also have the benefit of being able to look out of your side window when reversing round a right-hand corner.

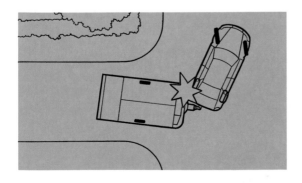

GETTING READY FOR WINTER

Winter puts extra strain on a car, and any minor problems which have been hiding are likely to become more obvious and cause trouble once winter gets a grip. In cold conditions, it takes more power to start the engine, and you'll be using the heater and demister more often – this takes its toll on the battery.

What to check before winter starts

Check the coolant mixture
If the coolant (antifreeze and water) freezes, it could wreck your engine. A garage can check the coolant for you, or you can buy a simple and inexpensive coolant tester. Except in an emergency, never fill your cooling system with plain water, even in summer – antifreeze stops corrosion inside the engine as well as protecting against the cold.

Check the drivebelt(s)
Look for damage, and check the tension of the belt(s). Refer to "Auxiliary drivebelts" for details.

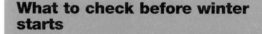

MAKING THE MOST OF YOUR **CAR**

Check the cooling system hoses
Look for signs of damage or leaks, and have any problem hoses renewed. Refer to "Leaks" for details of how to check and repair hoses.

Check the battery
Battery failure is the most common source of trouble in winter. Check that the battery is in good condition, then clean the battery lead connections, and make sure they're tight. If the battery shows signs that it might be getting towards the end of its life, fit a new one before winter starts. Refer to "Batteries" for details of how to check a battery.

Check the wipers and washers
You'll use them a lot more in winter. Make sure the wiper blades are in good condition (new ones aren't expensive, so it's well worth renewing them at the start of every winter anyway). Check the windscreen (and tailgate, if you have one) washer system.
Make sure the washer jets aren't blocked, and that they spray onto the screen, not over the top of the roof or onto the bonnet! Refer to "Screenwash fluid level check" for details. Always keep the washer fluid topped up.

Check all fluids and filters
Top up or renew if necessary. Refer to "Simple checks and servicing" for details.

Check all the lights and indicators
Make sure that they work properly, and replace any blown bulbs. Refer to "Bulb check" and "Lights and indicators" for details.

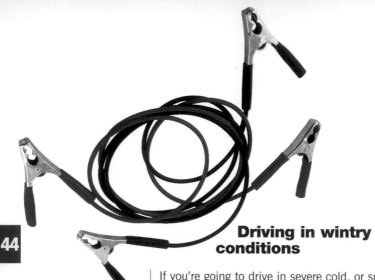

Driving in wintry conditions

If you're going to drive in severe cold, or snowy and icy conditions, make sure you're properly equipped. The weather can worsen very quickly in winter, so even if it looks OK when you set off, be prepared! When driving on slippery roads, drive slowly, smoothly and gently – accelerate gently, steer gently and brake gently.

Tell someone where you're going, what route you're taking and what time you're expecting to arrive at your destination.

Make sure you have a full tank of fuel – this will allow you to keep the engine running for warmth (through the heating system), without fear of running out of fuel, if you get delayed or stuck.

Carry warm clothes and blankets to keep you warm if you get stuck. A bar of chocolate could also come in handy.

Carry de-icer fluid, a scraper, jump leads and a tow rope.

Pack some pieces of old sacking, or similar material, which you can place under the wheels to give better traction if you get stuck.

Pack a shovel, in case you need to dig yourself out of trouble.

Use snow chains or studded tyres. In some areas, it's compulsory to use snow chains or studded tyres on certain roads (or even all roads!) – note, however, that it may also be compulsory to remove them again when you reach roads which are unaffected by ice or snow (this applies to many alpine roads at certain times of the year).

Windscreen de-icer spray

GETTING READY FOR A HOLIDAY

If you're taking your car on holiday, you want to be able to relax, so before you set off, it's a good idea to carry out all the checks mentioned in "What to check before winter starts" – this will reduce the possibility of any unexpected breakdowns. Make sure you're carrying all you need to get you out of trouble, particularly if you're travelling abroad – refer to "Things you should always carry" for details.

Don't overload your car. When you're loading, make sure any items you're likely to need during your journey (including your tool kit) are packed so that they're easily accessible.

Plan ahead

It's a good idea to plan your route before travelling, and have a good road map to hand. Many different maps and guides are available, and most of the motoring organisations will provide a set of directions to your destination, for a small charge, or sometimes free if you're a member. In some countries, you'll have to pay tolls to use certain roads.

If you're travelling a long way, make sure you allow time for any hold-ups, and make sure you take a break if you start to feel tired. If you're on a long journey and you have children in the car, make sure you can keep them amused.

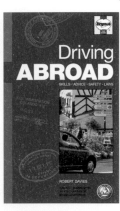

There is useful information in the book "Driving Abroad" to make your journey easier.

TRAVELLING ABROAD

Insurance

Check on the legal requirements for the country you're visiting, and always tell your insurance company that you're taking the car abroad. If you're travelling in the European Community (EC), most insurance policies automatically give only the minimum legally-required cover. If you want the same level of cover as you have at home, you'll usually have to obtain an internationally-recognised certificate of insurance ("Green card"), often for a small charge.

It's a good idea to take out medical insurance. Not all countries have a free emergency medical service, and you could find yourself faced with a large unexpected bill. With a travel insurance policy, you're usually covered for any money lost if you have to cancel your holiday, and your luggage may also be covered against loss or theft. Make sure you take time to read the small print so that you know exactly what's covered!

Recovery and breakdown costs can be far higher abroad. Most of the motoring organisations will be able to provide insurance cover which could save you a lot of inconvenience and expense if you break down.

Driving laws

Make sure you're familiar with the driving laws in the country you're visiting – the penalties for breaking the law may be severe! You may be legally required to carry certain safety equipment such as spare light bulbs, a warning triangle and a first aid kit. If you're driving on the opposite side of the road from normal, you'll need to fit headlight beam deflectors to avoid dazzling other drivers. Make sure that you know the appropriate speed limits, and note that in some countries, there's an absolute ban on driving after drinking any alcohol.

Fuel

The type and quality of fuel available varies from country to country. Check on availability, and find out what fuel pump markings to look for to give you the correct type and grade of fuel for your car.

Documents

Always carry your passport, driving licence, vehicle registration document, vehicle test certificate, and insurance certificate(s) (including medical and breakdown insurance, where applicable).

Make sure that all the documents are valid, and that the car tax and vehicle test certificate don't run out whilst you're abroad.

Before travelling, check in case any special documents or permits are required. You may need a visa to visit some countries, and an international driving permit (available from the major motoring organisations) may be required.

SAFETY

Road accidents claim thousands of lives every year. The genuine accident which is nobody's fault and could not have been avoided is in fact very rare. Most accidents don't happen, they are caused. Young drivers have more than their share of incidents, due to a combination of inexperience and bravado, which is why their insurance premiums are so high.

Working on your car is nothing like as dangerous as driving it, but it can still be risky if you are unaware of particular hazards. This chapter sets out to encourage a safety-conscious attitude, which can and should be applied to almost every activity you undertake.

Child seats

Child seats must conform to national safety standards and be fixed in accordance with their maker's instructions – usually by means of existing seat belts (see "Carrying Children").

SEAT BELTS

The risk of serious injury if you have an accident is much higher if you travel without the seat belts fastened.

There are a few things to think about when wearing a seat belt:

◆ The seat belt webbing mustn't be twisted.
◆ The upper part of the belt must pass diagonally across the wearer's shoulder and chest.
◆ The lower part of the belt must fit closely across the wearer's hips, not the abdomen!
◆ Don't use any clips or fasteners which prevent the belt from touching the wearer's body.
◆ NEVER travel with a child sitting on a passenger's lap.

◆ **Check the seat belts occasionally (for instance, when the car is serviced) as follows:**
◆ Check that the webbing is not twisted.
◆ Check that the belts are not cut or fraying, and that they retract freely.
◆ If the webbing is dirty, clean it using soapy water, then allow it to dry in the shade. NEVER use strong detergents, bleach, or chemicals, and make sure that the retractors don't get wet.
◆ After even a moderate impact, have the seat belts replaced. Many cars have seat belt tensioners which pull the belt tight against the wearer if there's an impact. If the tensioner mechanism has been activated, the seat belt must be renewed.

SAFETY

SAFETY WHEN YOU'RE CHECKING YOUR CAR

Working on your car can be dangerous, so this page shows just some of the possible risks and hazards, to help you avoid any mishaps or injuries.

Do

- wear eye protection.
- wear gloves or use barrier cream.
- get someone to periodically check that all is well.
- keep clothing, etc, well out of the way of moving parts.
- remove rings, watch, etc, before working on the car.
- ensure that any lifting equipment is adequate.
- mop up fluid spills immediately.

Don't

- try to lift a component which might be too heavy.
- rush to finish a job, or try to take shortcuts.
- use poorly-fitting tools which might slip.
- leave tools or parts lying around.

Asbestos

Asbestos dust is cancerous if inhaled or swallowed. Asbestos may be found in gaskets and in brake and clutch linings.

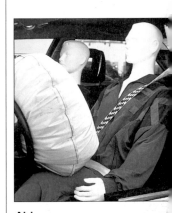

Airbags

Airbags can cause injury if they go off accidentally.

Leaks

Never drive the car if you think there may be a fuel leak – leaking fuel, or fuel vapour could be ignited by the hot exhaust or engine components, which can cause a rapid and serious fire or even an explosion.

Refer to "Leaks" for details of what to do if you think there might be a fuel leak.

Very hot
water

Scalding
- Don't remove the coolant filler cap while the engine's hot.
- When draining oil or fluid, remember that it may be hot.

DANGER
Hot

Burning
- Beware of burns from the exhaust system and from any part of the engine. Brake components can also be extremely hot after use.
- All types of air conditioning refrigerant can cause skin burns.

DANGER
Petroleum
mixture
giving off a
flammable
heavy vapour

Fire
- Don't let fuel spill onto a hot engine or manifold. Don't smoke or allow naked lights (including pilot lights) anywhere near a car being worked on. Also beware of creating sparks.
- Fuel vapour is heavier than air, so don't work on the fuel system with the car over an inspection pit.
- The commonest cause of vehicle fires is an electrical overload or short-circuit. Take care when repairing or modifying the vehicle wiring.
- Keep a fire extinguisher of a suitable type handy.

DANGER
Electric shock
risk

Electric shock
- Don't work on the ignition system with the engine running or the ignition switched on.
- Make sure that any mains-operated equipment is earthed, when applicable. Mains power points should be protected by a circuit breaker.

SAFETY

Fume or gas intoxication

- Exhaust fumes are poisonous. Never run the engine in a confined space such as a garage with the doors shut.
- Fuel vapour is also poisonous, as are the vapours from some cleaning solvents and paint thinners.

DANGER
Harmful fumes

Poisonous or irritant substances

- Avoid skin contact with battery acid and with any fuel, fluid or lubricant, especially antifreeze, brake hydraulic fluid and diesel fuel.
- Wear gloves or use a barrier cream if contact with oil is expected.
- Some types of air conditioning refrigerant form a poisonous gas if exposed to a naked flame (including a cigarette).

Dangerous
substance

The battery

- Batteries contain sulphuric acid, which is poisonous and corrosive.
- The hydrogen gas given off by the battery is highly explosive.
- When charging or jump starting, observe any special precautions specified by the battery maker.

Crushing

- Don't take risks when working under or near a raised car.
- Take extra care if loosening or tightening nuts or bolts when the car is on stands.
- In an emergency such as roadside wheel changing, slide the spare wheel under the car to provide some support if the jack slips.

SAFETY WHEN YOU'RE DRIVING

These days, car manufacturers are paying more attention to safety. Many cars are fitted with safety devices such as side impact protection bars, seat belt tensioners and airbags, but it's still down to the driver to avoid having an accident in the first place!

You can reduce the risk of being involved in an accident when driving just by being aware of some of the risks which can be avoided.

Before starting a journey

It's important to make sure that you're comfortable, and that you can concentrate on driving without any unnecessary distractions. Make sure that your seat is comfortably positioned, and that the rear view mirrors are adjusted so that you have a clear view behind the car. If the car has an adjustable steering column, adjust it so that the wheel can be reached comfortably, and turned easily without stretching.

Check that you can see clearly through the windscreen and windows – clean the glass if necessary, and in winter, if the car windows are iced up or covered in snow, don't drive the car until they're clear.

Check that there are no distracting reflections in the windscreen or rear window.

If you're tired, or if you've been drinking alcohol recently, or taking medication, are you fit to drive? These can all reduce your co-ordination, increase your reaction time, and affect your judgement. Don't take any chances!

Finally, before you set off, check that all your passengers are comfortable.

SAFETY

During a journey

When you're on a journey it can sometimes be very difficult to maintain concentration, especially on a motorway, when there's no need to change gear or brake, and all you have to do is steer.

Concentrate and think ahead
- always be prepared for the unexpected.
- drive at a safe speed to suit road conditions.
- don't break the speed limit.

Slow down
- in heavy traffic or bad weather conditions.

Don't drive too close to the vehicle in front
- multiple pile-ups on motorways are usually caused by vehicles driving too fast, and following each other too closely.

Use your mirrors regularly
- you need to know what's happening behind you as well as in front.

Always signal your manoeuvres clearly and in plenty of time
- check your mirrors first, and don't make any sudden moves.

Stop as soon as possible if you feel tired
- wind down a window for fresh air, and turn down the heater. If you feel tired on a motorway, stop at the next service station, or turn off at the next junction – don't stop on the hard shoulder unless it's an emergency.

Stay calm
- if other drivers annoy you, or seem to be annoyed with you. "Road rage" is now a significant problem. Don't be drawn into a confrontation, and if someone starts following you, head for a busy town centre, or a police station – don't try to drive fast to "shake off" your pursuer, and don't drive to your home. If you have to stop, lock all the car doors and close the windows, and stay inside the car.

If you break down . . .
refer to "What to do if you break down".

If you're involved in an accident . . .
refer to "What to do at the scene of an accident".

TROUBLE-
SHOOTING

Modern cars are much more reliable than those of 20 years ago, so it's to be hoped that you won't need to use this chapter very often. It contains advice on identifying fluid leaks, diagnosing nasty noises and establishing what the problem is if your car won't start or stops suddenly. Perhaps more importantly, it also explains when you can carry on driving and when it would be unwise, or even dangerous, to do so. If you have your car serviced regularly and keep an eye on tyres, fluid levels, hoses and drivebelts, you've gone a long way towards avoiding any problems.

PROBLEMS WITH DIESEL

Cold weather problems

Diesel sold in cold conditions is different to that sold when the weather's warmer. This is because diesel fuel goes "waxy" when it gets cold, and can even freeze - additives are used in cold weather to try to reduce problems. Most diesel engine cars have a fuel heater, which warms the fuel before it goes into the engine – this normally stops problems in cold weather. If you do have problems due to fuel waxing, the only thing you can do is warm the engine, or wait for the weather to warm up – never use a naked flame to warm an engine. The best solution is to park the car in a garage, and use an electric heater to warm the engine.

Water in fuel

Diesel cars usually have a water separator, and one of the regular maintenance jobs is to drain off the water – if water gets into the fuel system, it can cause corrosion. Make sure that you drain off water from the separator at the recommended intervals, or more often if necessary – this will avoid problems.

PROBLEMS WITH PETROL

Any problems with petrol are usually due to contamination, which can cause engine running problems. If you think the petrol may be contaminated, see if the problem is still there after you next fill up - if it is, have the fuel system checked. Most cars that can run only on unleaded petrol have a small fuel filler neck – the wrong pump nozzle won't fit, so you can't fill up with the wrong fuel!

SUSPENSION PROBLEMS

If the suspension components are worn or damaged, you'll probably notice that the handling and ride will suffer, and you may notice noises and rattles, especially when driving over bumps. Worn suspension components can also cause increased tyre wear, and poor braking.

The suspension components are very accurately aligned, and even a small tap to a wheel from "kerbing" can knock out the alignment and cause tyre wear. Many tyre specialists will be able to check the alignment for you.

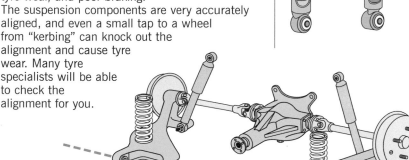

How to check shock absorbers

Press down and then release each corner of the car in turn. The corner of the car should move back up to its original position, and then settle. If the suspension rises up and bounces when you let go, or if you hear a hissing or knocking sound as the suspension moves, the shock absorber is probably faulty.

STEERING PROBLEMS

Basically, the same comments made under "Suspension problems" apply to the steering. The most common problem is poor front wheel alignment, which can cause tyre wear (see "Tyre wear").

Worn steering components can cause excessive free play at the steering wheel, and if you notice this problem, it should be dealt with as soon as possible.

Problems with power steering are usually due to leaks or air in the hydraulic system, or an incorrectly adjusted or broken pump drivebelt. If the power steering fails, the steering will still work, but the steering wheel will be harder to turn.

If you think there may be a problem with the steering, have it checked as soon as possible – never take any risks where the steering is concerned.

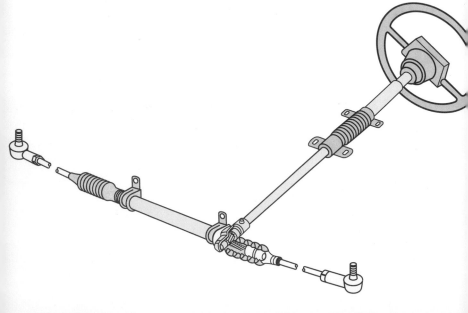

TROUBLESHOOTING

LEAKS

A leak may show up as a stain under your car, or you may be forever topping-up one of the fluids (see "Simple checks and servicing"). So how do you tell if a leak is serious, or something you can live with for a while?

Apart from an obvious pool of liquid under your car, if you have to top up any of the fluids regularly, this may also indicate a leak. If you have to top up the engine oil regularly, the engine could be burning oil – see "All about oil".

Brake Fluid

Symptoms
Brake fluid is clear, thin and almost watery. Old brake fluid gradually darkens. Compare the leak with the contents of the brake fluid reservoir. Leaks usually come from around the wheels, the brake line connections under the car, or the brake master cylinder in the engine compartment.

Is it OK to drive the car?
DON'T drive the car if you think there might be a brake fluid leak.

Is it easy to fix?
Dismantling will be required to fix this, call for help.

Clutch Fluid

Symptoms
Leaks usually come from hydraulic line connections, or from failed seals in the hydraulic components.

Is it OK to drive the car?
It's OK to drive with a minor leak, but if you lose all the fluid, the clutch won't work.

Is it easy to fix?
You might be able to fix a leaky fluid line union by tightening it. The leak could be due to a failed fluid seal in one of the clutch hydraulic components. Dismantling will be required to fix this – call for help.

Automatic transmission fluid

Symptoms

The fluid may be clear or a reddish-brown colour. Compare the leak with the fluid on the end of the transmission fluid level dipstick. Leaks usually come from the transmission casing, or from fluid lines running to the fluid cooler (this could be mounted on the transmission, or incorporated in the radiator).

Is it OK to drive the car?

You can drive with a minor leak, but keep an eye on the fluid level.

Is it easy to fix?

You might be able to fix a leaky connection by tightening it. Any other leaks should be checked out by a garage.

Engine oil

Symptoms

Engine oil is usually black, unless it's recently been changed. Clean oil is usually clear or green. Compare the leak with the oil on the end of the oil level dipstick. The most common sources of leaks are the oil drain plug, the oil filter, and the sump gasket under the engine.

Is it OK to drive the car?

You can drive with a minor oil leak, but keep an eye on the oil level.

Is it easy to fix?

If the leak's coming from the oil drain plug or the filter, try tightening the plug or filter (as applicable). If the leak's coming from anywhere else, have it checked as soon as possible.

Manual transmission or final drive oil

Symptoms

The oil is usually a tan colour or reddish-pink, although old oil may darken. Transmission oil is thicker than engine oil, and often has a very sickly smell, especially when hot.

Is it OK to drive the car?

You can drive with a minor leak, but if the oil level gets too low, it can cause serious transmission damage.

Is it easy to fix?

Most leaks are due to failed gaskets or oil seals, so dismantling is usually required to fix the leak – get a garage to have a look as soon as you can.

Petrol

Symptoms

Petrol has a strong and distinctive smell, so a leak should be obvious. If you've just filled up with petrol on a hot day, and the car's standing in the sun, the petrol may expand, and leak out through the fuel tank breather. Petrol can also leak if you park a car with a full tank on a steep slope.

If the leak's not due to either of the above causes, have it investigated straight away.

Is it OK to drive the car?

DON'T drive the car until the leak's been fixed.

Is it easy to fix?

If the leak's coming from a hose connection, you might be able to cure it by tightening the connection (or hose clip) – if not, don't try to fix the leak yourself, call for help.

Diesel fuel

Symptoms

Diesel fuel has a distinctive oily smell (like domestic heating oil), and is a clear, oily substance. As with petrol, a recently filled tank may leak a little due to expansion. Any other leak is cause for concern.

Is it OK to drive the car?

DON'T drive the car until the leak's been fixed.

Is it easy to fix?

If the leak's coming from a fuel line connection, you might be able to cure it by tightening the connection (or hose clip); if not, don't try to fix the leak yourself, call for help.

Washer fluid

Symptoms

Washer fluid usually contains a coloured dye, and has a strong smell of detergent, alcohol or ammonia. The leak could be due to a poor pipe connection, or a leaky washer pump seal in the fluid reservoir.

Is it OK to drive the car?

Yes!

Is it easy to fix?

Yes, but it might be tricky to get to the fluid pipes and reservoir.

Coolant

Symptoms
Coolant usually contains a bright-coloured dye, and has a strong, sickly sweet smell. Old coolant may be rusty or dirty brown, and there may be a white crystalline deposit around the leak. Leaks usually come from a hose, the radiator, or the heater inside the car (you'll smell coolant when you switch the heater on).

Is it OK to drive the car?
You can drive with a minor leak, but if you lose too much coolant, the engine could overheat.

Is it easy to fix?
Sometimes you can stop a leak by tightening up a hose clip. If a hose is split, you might be able to make an emergency repair using a repair bandage. If the radiator or heater is leaking, you may be able to fix it temporarily by using a radiator sealant.

Water
If a leak looks like clear water, and your car has air conditioning, it may not be a leak, but condensation from the air conditioning. A lot of condensation can be produced on a hot day, which may look like a major leak. Also see "Coolant" and "Washer fluid".

Power Steering Fluid

Symptoms
The fluid is usually clear or reddish-brown. Compare the leak with the contents of the power steering fluid reservoir. Leaks usually come from fluid line connections, the power steering pump, or the steering gear.

Is it OK to drive the car?
You can drive with a minor leak, but keep an eye on the fluid level.

Is it easy to fix?
To fix a leaky fluid line connection, try tightening it. If the pump or steering gear is leaking, you'll need advice from a garage.

Shock absorber fluid

Symptoms
Usually shows up as a dark stain on the shock absorber body.

Is it OK to drive the car?
Yes, but you may have a poor ride, and poor handling – take care!

Is it easy to fix?
You'll need two new shock absorbers – ie, if one rear shock absorber is leaking, you should renew both rear shock absorbers. Consult a garage or a fast-fit specialist.

Grease

Symptoms
Grease is usually black or grey, thick and very sticky! You may find it under the car if it's leaked from the driveshaft rubber gaiters or steering gear gaiters.

Is it OK to drive the car?
Yes, but if much grease has been lost, the driveshaft or steering gear could be damaged through lack of lubrication.

Is it easy to fix?
Some dismantling will be required, so consult a garage.

WHAT'S THAT NOISE?

A strange noise could spell trouble, or it could just be an annoying distraction – so how do you tell? Here's a guide to help you to identify noises and decide what to do about them, even if you just want to describe the problem to a mechanic.

Noise	Possible cause	Remarks
Noises from the exhaust		
Light "puffing" or blowing noise when accelerating or decelerating, or when engine is idling	Small hole or crack in exhaust system	Repair temporarily with exhaust putty. Go to exhaust specialist for advice.
Sudden increase in noise, especially when accelerating and decelerating	Hole or crack in exhaust system, or failed silencer	Repair temporarily with exhaust bandage. Go to exhaust specialist for advice.
Metallic rattling or thumping over bumps, or when accelerating and decelerating	Loose or broken exhaust mounting	Repair temporarily with wire. Go to exhaust specialist for advice.
Noises from the brakes		
Light squeaking when applying brakes gently for the first time of the day	Normal characteristic of disc brakes	Could be normal.
Squealing whenever brakes are applied	Could be first sign of excessively worn brake friction material	Ask your garage to check – possibly cured by applying special brake grease to the metal brake component surfaces. Renew brake pads or shoes if required.
Deep metallic scraping when brakes are applied, or when the brakes aren't in use	Excessively worn brake components. Trapped stone or dirt between brake disc and pad	Have your garage investigate without delay before further damage occurs.
Chattering or tapping when brakes are applied	Contaminated brake friction material	Damaged brake discs or drums. Have your garage investigate without delay.

TROUBLESHOOTING

Noise	Possible cause	Remarks
Noises from the suspension		
Clunks or rattles when driving over bumps	Worn or damaged suspension or steering components. Loose or broken exhaust mounting	Probably not urgent, but have your garage investigate before too long.
Rumbling, growling or clicking noises when turning corners	Worn wheel bearing(s) Worn driveshaft joint (front-wheel-drive cars)	Probably not urgent, but may cause further damage if neglected.
"Hissing" noise when driving slowly over bumps	Badly worn shock absorbers	Drive carefully until new shock absorbers have been fitted - handling and ride may be poor.
Constant clicking noise	Stone embedded in tyre Wheel fouling brake or suspension component	Take the stone out with your penknife! If it's not a stone, seek advice.
Noises from the engine compartment		
Squealing	Loose or worn auxiliary drivebelt or timing belt	Probably not urgent, but get it fixed before it breaks.
Continuous hum or whine	Auxiliary drivebelt or timing belt too tight Alternator, coolant pump or power steering pump worn	Probably not urgent, but get it fixed before it gets worse.
Rhythmic slapping when the engine is cold	"Piston slap"	Not a problem as long as it stops when engine warms up.
Light tapping from the top of the engine	Valve clearances incorrect (too large)	Not urgent, but have them adjusted at the next service.
Rhythmic metallic thumping or thudding	Worn engine bearings or camshaft	May be a serious problem. Have it investigated without delay.
High-pitched metallic rattle when engine is under load (accelerating or driving uphill)	Engine "pinking" or "pre-ignition" (poor quality fuel or wrong fuel type, or ignition system fault)	Drive gently until you can fill up with good fuel or have the ignition system checked.

Noise	Possible cause	Remarks
Noises from the transmission		
Whine or howl from manual transmission in neutral, quietens or disappears when clutch pedal is depressed	Worn transmission bearing	You can still drive, but have it fixed before it gets much worse.
Whine or howl from manual transmission when clutch pedal is depressed, quietens or disappears when pedal is released	Worn clutch release bearing	You can still drive, but have it fixed before it gets much worse.
Squealing from manual transmission as clutch is engaged or released	Incorrectly adjusted clutch Worn clutch	If adjustment doesn't cure the problem, have it fixed before it gets worse.
Whine or howl from automatic transmission in neutral	Low transmission fluid level Worn or damaged transmission	Check the fluid level. If that's OK, have the transmission checked without delay.
Howl or whine when accelerating or decelerating	Low transmission oil/fluid level Worn bearing in transmission Worn or damaged differential	Check the oil level. If that's OK, you can probably carry on driving for a while, but have the transmission checked before something breaks.
"Graunching" sound from manual transmission when changing gear	Incorrectly adjusted clutch Worn synchromesh units in transmission Badly worn gear teeth	If clutch adjustment doesn't cure it, you probably need a new transmission.

WHY DID IT STOP?

Although there isn't space here to give a comprehensive fault-finding guide, if the engine stops, it's useful to have some idea of where to start looking for the problem.

If the engine stops running suddenly as if the ignition has been switched off, it's probably due to an ignition system fault, whereas if the engine splutters or misfires before finally stopping, it's usually a fuel system fault. The following chart will give you a few clues.

Symptom	Possible cause
Engine suddenly stops as if switched off	Faulty ignition switch (or switch accidentally turned off!) Loose or broken connection or wire in ignition system Faulty ignition system component(s) Loose or broken battery earth connection
Engine splutters or misfires, loses power and stops	Fuel tank empty! Fuel cut-off switch activated (see "What to do if your car won't start") Dirt or water in fuel lines Faulty fuel system component(s) Water on ignition system components (in bad weather or after going through a flood) Faulty ignition system component(s)
Engine makes unpleasant noises and stops	Mechanical failure (such as broken timing belt)

WHY WON'T IT START?

If the engine won't start, work through the following flow chart to try to find a clue to the cause – you may not be able to fix the problem yourself, but at least you'll be able to give a mechanic a few clues about the cause of the problem.

Does the starter motor turn? — NO — Switch the headlights on —

YES

Does the starter motor turn the engine? — NO —
- Faulty starter motor
- Engine fault

YES

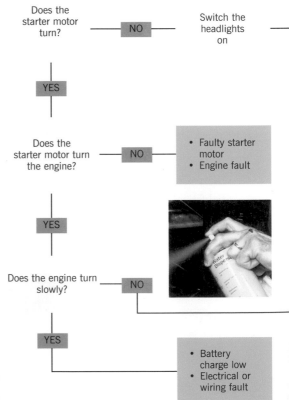

Does the engine turn slowly? — NO —

YES
- Battery charge low
- Electrical or wiring fault

Do the lights
come on? — NO →
- Flat battery
- Loose, dirty or corroded battery terminals
- Other electrical or wiring fault

 YES

Do the lights
dim when you try to — NO →
start the engine?
- Loose or dirty starter motor connections
- Faulty starter motor or ignition switch
- Automatic transmission gear selector lever not in 'N' or 'P'
- Other electrical or wiring fault

 YES

- Battery charge low
- Loose, dirty or corroded battery connections
- Faulty starter motor
- Other electrical or wiring fault
- Seized engine

- Fuel tank empty
- Dirty or loose ignition system components – petrol engines
- Incorrectly adjusted or faulty spark plugs – petrol engines
- Air in fuel lines – diesel engines
- Dirt in fuel lines
- Fuel system fault
- Other electrical or wiring fault

IN AN EMERGENCY

Nobody sets off in their car intending to break down or have an accident. Punctures are much rarer than they used to be, laminated windscreens don't shatter and even running out of fuel is easier to avoid now that most cars have low fuel level warning lights. Car crime, on the other hand, is a persistent problem almost everywhere.

The following pages contain some useful advice on what to do in various emergency situations. Most of it is common sense, but it's probably worth reading through it at leisure to make sure that you would know what to do in any of the situations mentioned.

*Note:
Sometimes two or more of the brake warning lights are combined. If you suspect that the light may indicate low brake fluid level, DO NOT drive the car until you've checked the level, topped up if necessary, and checked for leaks.

WARNING LIGHTS

Your car is fitted with various warning lights to warn you of faults or possible problems with your car's systems. Some warnings are more serious than others, so here's a guide as to what the more common warning lights mean, and what to do if they come on.

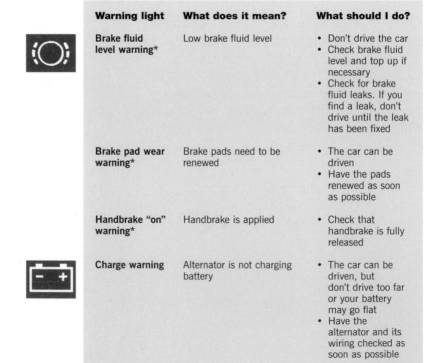

	Warning light	What does it mean?	What should I do?
	Brake fluid level warning*	Low brake fluid level	• Don't drive the car • Check brake fluid level and top up if necessary • Check for brake fluid leaks. If you find a leak, don't drive until the leak has been fixed
	Brake pad wear warning*	Brake pads need to be renewed	• The car can be driven • Have the pads renewed as soon as possible
	Handbrake "on" warning*	Handbrake is applied	• Check that handbrake is fully released
	Charge warning	Alternator is not charging battery	• The car can be driven, but don't drive too far or your battery may go flat • Have the alternator and its wiring checked as soon as possible

IN AN EMERGENCY

Warning light	What does it mean?	What should I do?	
Oil pressure warning	Engine oil pressure low	• If light comes on when engine is idling – worn or very hot engine. Check that the light goes out when you "blip" the throttle. • Check the oil level as soon as possible. • If the light comes on when driving – stop the engine immediately, check the oil level and look for oil leaks, then call for assistance if necessary. Serious damage could be caused if you run the engine	
Coolant temperature warning	Coolant temperature excessive	• Stop as soon as possible. Allow the engine to cool, then check the coolant level; top up if necessary. • If the light comes on again within a short distance, stop and call for assistance	
Coolant level warning	Engine coolant level low	• Stop as soon as possible. Allow the engine to cool, then check the coolant level; top up if necessary. • If the light comes on again within a short distance, check for leaks	

Warning light	What does it mean?	What should I do?
Engine system warning	Fault code stored in engine management self-diagnostic system	• The car can be driven, but you may notice a loss of performance. Have the engine management system checked as soon as possible
ABS warning	ABS fault	• The car can be driven, but the ABS may not be working (normal braking will not be affected). Have the ABS tested as soon as possible
Airbag (or SRS) warning	Airbag system fault	• The car can be driven, but the airbag system may not work in the event of an accident. Have the airbag system checked as soon as possible
Glow plug warning (diesel)	Glow plugs operating	• Wait for the light to go out before trying to start the engine
Choke warning (petrol)	Choke is applied	• Push the choke control in once the engine has warmed up – the light will then go out
Water in fuel warning (diesel)	Water needs to be drained from the fuel filter	• Refer to "Fuel filter draining and renewal – diesel engines"
Low fuel warning	Low fuel level in tank	• Fill up soon

IN AN EMERGENCY

WHAT TO DO IF YOU BREAK DOWN

If you're unfortunate enough to break down on the road, try to keep calm, and think logically. You may not know what's wrong, but don't panic – the majority of breakdowns are caused by simple problems, which can easily be fixed at the roadside by a good mechanic.

The following advice has been written with women driving alone particularly in mind, but much of it applies to any driver.

On ordinary roads

Try to stop where there are other people about. If possible, move the car out of the way of other traffic, then switch on the hazard warning lights, and set up your warning triangle if you have one. Lift up the bonnet – this will indicate to other motorists and any passing police patrol vehicles that you have a problem.

NEVER hitch a lift.

If you need to walk to a phone, take any children with you. Give details of:

1. Your location
2. Your car make, colour and registration number
3. The likely cause of the breakdown, or any symptoms
4. Whether you're alone, or with young children
5. Your motoring organisation membership number (if applicable)

Don't worry if you don't have all this information. Return to your car and, unless there's a danger of other traffic hitting it, stay inside, lock the doors, close the windows, and wait for help.

If someone stops to offer help, talk to them through a closed window until you're absolutely sure that you can trust them. ALWAYS ask for identification. It must be a personal decision to accept help – or not.

Breakdown assistance

Although it may seem expensive at first glance, joining one of the breakdown assistance organisations is very worthwhile, and could save you a lot of hassle and money. If you break down, and you don't belong to one of the motoring organisations, you'll have to arrange for roadside assistance, or recovery to a garage – this will almost certainly cost you more than a year's membership fee! Even if you only choose the basic minimum membership package from one of the leading motoring organisations, you'll easily save more than your membership fee the first time you have to call on their services. Some organisations will give you the option of being transported to your intended destination, or back home and, for an additional fee, will also provide breakdown cover if you take your car abroad. There's also the "peace-of-mind" factor when you know that help is never far away.

On a motorway

Pull onto the hard shoulder and park well away from the main carriageway. Switch on the hazard warning lights. If you don't have a mobile phone, get out of the car using the passenger's side door (taking any children with you) and walk to the nearest emergency telephone, keeping well in to the side of the hard shoulder. Arrows on marker posts at the edge of the hard shoulder indicate the direction to the nearest emergency phone – the phones will link you to a control centre. When you use the phone, face oncoming traffic.

If you do have a mobile phone, get out of the car using the passenger's side door (again, take any children with you), then use your phone to contact your motoring organisation or the police.

Tell the operator on the other end of the phone:

1. Your exact location (the emergency phones on a motorway are numbered)
2. Your car make, colour and registration number
3. The likely cause of the breakdown, or any symptoms
4. Whether you're alone, or with young children
5. Your motoring organisation membership number (if applicable)

Don't worry if you don't have all this information. Return to your car, but stand well away, and don't get in unless you feel at risk – fatal accidents occur on the hard shoulder.

IN AN EMERGENCY

TOP 10 BREAKDOWNS
(and how to avoid them)

1 Battery failure
Battery problems are the biggest single source of call-outs. The electrical systems on modern cars make heavy demands on the battery. Autumn, after the clocks have gone back, is the peak time for problems as colder weather and increased use of headlights combine to push elderly batteries over the edge.

What you can do to avoid problems:
• Keep battery terminals free of corrosion (spray with WD-40 or similar).
• Keep the top of the battery clean and dry.
• Check the alternator drivebelt now and again.
• Have the battery and charging system tested at the first sign of any problems (difficult starting, dim headlights, charging system warning light on).
• Carry a set of jump leads and know how to use them (see "How to use jump leads").
• Start the engine before switching on the headlights, and remember to turn the lights off when you leave the vehicle!

2 Electrical problem (not ignition or battery)
This covers a multitude of possibilities, from a blown light bulb to a major malfunction in the engine management system.

What you can do to avoid electrical problems generally:
• Look after the battery (see above).
• Spray exposed electrical connectors with WD-40, or similar, occasionally.
• Have any electrical problems investigated before they become serious.
• Carry spare fuses and light bulbs, and learn how to change them yourself.

3 Flat tyre

Many people will change a flat tyre themselves - if they know how and if they don't run into problems. Doing it yourself may well be quicker than waiting for assistance. Be extra vigilant on the motorway hard shoulder, both for yourself and for your passengers.

What you can do to avoid problems:
• Check tyre pressures and condition regularly (see "Tyre checks"). This includes the spare!
• Carry a jack and wheel nut spanner, and perhaps an 'instant repair' aerosol.
• Practise changing a wheel (see "How to change a wheel"), if need be with the help of a friend.

4 Flood damage

This one has moved up the charts recently, with some drivers learning the very expensive lesson that water drawn into the engine cannot be compressed, so something will break. Diesels are most vulnerable to this kind of damage, but no engine takes kindly to a forced diet of flood water.

What you can do to avoid problems:
• Don't drive into flood water of unknown depth. If possible, watch and see what happens to other vehicles first.
• In water which can be negotiated, proceed slowly but keep the engine running fairly fast (2000–3000 rpm). Slip the clutch if necessary.
• Once back on dry land, try your brakes. If they are weak or pull to one side, keep re-applying them until they dry out. If the brakes make odd noises or don't seem to be working well, have them investigated.
• If the inside of the car got wet, dry it out without delay.

IN AN **EMERGENCY**

5 Run out of fuel

If you're not a member of a motoring organisation, this may cost you dearly. Carrying a spare can of fuel is potentially hazardous; if you choose to do so, only use an approved container, securely fastened.

What you can do to avoid problems:
- Before setting out on a journey, make sure that you have sufficient fuel in the tank, or that you know where and how to get some more *en route*.
- Keep an eye on the fuel gauge and fill up as soon as it gets much below the quarter-full mark.
- Fill up immediately if the "low fuel" warning light comes on – but don't feel you have to wait for the light!

6 Overheating

Not surprisingly, summer is the peak time for overheating, with heavily loaded vehicles struggling to keep cool in slow traffic or on long uphill stretches. Beware of scalding if you have to top up the coolant.

What you can do to avoid problems:
- Check coolant level before a long journey; look for leaks if the level is low.
- Change the coolant at least every two years (or as recommended by the car manufacturer).
- At the first sign of overheating, switch the heater and heater blower to maximum. Open the windows too!
- Don't continue to drive with the temperature gauge in the red or the warning light on.

7 Clutch problems

There are two possible problems with the clutch: it may slip (engine speed rises but car speed doesn't) or it may drag (gears crunch and are hard or impossible to engage; clutch pedal may be low or on the floor). The problem may be nothing more than a broken or sticking cable, or it could be more serious.

What you can do to avoid problems:
- Periodically check clutch fluid level or cable condition and adjustment (as applicable).
- Be alert to signs of problems and have them investigated before they cause a roadside breakdown.

8 Brake problems

An illuminated ABS warning light can safely be ignored until you can reach your own servicing garage. A brake pad wear warning light is also not a reason to call for assistance, provided you act on it before the pads wear down to the metal. Any other problems with the braking system should be taken very seriously. Don't drive on unless you are sure it is safe to do so.

What you can do to avoid problems:
- Check the brake fluid level from time to time and investigate any sudden fall.
- Inspect brake pads and shoes at least once a year (or as specified), and renew as necessary.
- On automatics, do use the handbrake occasionally to stop it seizing up.
- Remember prevention is better than cure - failure to renew a set of brake pads in time can mean you have to fit new discs as well, at much greater expense.

9 Ignition system problems

Modern ignition systems are very reliable; generally they work well or not at all, and a roadside repair may not be possible. However it is always worth trying the effect of squirting WD-40 or equivalent over the spark plug leads, coil(s) and connectors, especially if conditions are damp or wet. Take precautions against electric shock before touching spark plug leads - switch off the ignition and remove the key.

What you can do to avoid problems:
* Keep spark plug leads and ignition coil(s) clean and dry.
* Renew spark plugs at the specified intervals; check the leads at the same time.
* Buy a diesel-engined car (no spark plugs to worry about).

10 Timing belt failure

Unheard of 30 years ago, the timing belt is most definitely a mixed blessing. Certain prestigious manufacturers have never used them - for the rest of us, once the belt has broken it is at least inconvenient (recovery to a garage will be needed) and at worst disastrous (the engine may be damaged beyond repair).

What you can do to avoid problems:
* Ideally, don't buy a car with an engine which has a timing belt.
* If the engine does have a timing belt, renew it at or before the specified interval.
* When buying a second-hand car, have the timing belt renewed without delay unless there is proof that it has been done recently.

WHAT TO DO IF YOU'VE LOCKED YOURSELF OUT OF YOUR CAR

How serious this is will depend on how easy your car is to break into. If you are not acquainted with any professional car thieves you will have to call a breakdown organisation, or break in yourself. Some damage may be caused whichever method you choose.

What you can do to avoid problems:
• Carry a spare set of keys.
• Make a note of key numbers so that replacements can be ordered.
• Don't leave keys inside the vehicle, even if not intending to lock it. (Some central locking systems set themselves automatically after a short interval.)
• Don't put keys down in the luggage area or on the rear shelf - it's only too easy to close the boot lid or tailgate and lock the keys inside.

Hiding a spare set of keys on the vehicle has obvious advantages, but your insurance company will take a dim view of the practice if the car is stolen as a result.

HOW TO CHANGE A WHEEL

Changing a wheel is straightforward provided you know where the tools and spare wheel are kept, and how to use the jack. If you've just bought the car, or if you've never changed a wheel before, it's worth practising at home, then you'll know exactly what to do if you get a flat tyre.

1 Apply the handbrake, engage first gear (set automatic transmission to "P"), then chock the wheel diagonally opposite the one to be changed.

2 Get out the spare wheel, vehicle jack and wheelbrace. They are generally located in the luggage area, under a cover in the floor (check your car's handbook for details).

3 Where applicable, remove the wheel trim/cover. Use the wheelbrace to loosen each wheel bolt/nut on the affected wheel by about half a turn.

Be Safe
If you get a flat tyre when you're on a journey, first make sure that the car is parked safely away from traffic. If you're at the side of a busy road, and you can't move the car, it's safer to call for assistance rather than risk an accident. Stop the car, switch on the hazard warning lights, and set up your warning triangle if you have one.

Sometimes it's difficult to loosen the wheel bolts or nuts. You can buy a wheel brace with an extending handle to make things easier, or alternatively, you can carry a length of metal tube to fit over the wheel brace for more leverage.

Fitting a wheel

Positioning a wheel on the hub can be tricky, as you have to support its weight at the same time. If you find this difficult, try resting the wheel on your foot and using it to help you manoeuvre the wheel into position.

4 Engage the jack head in the jacking point nearest the affected wheel (check your car's handbook for details). Slide the spare wheel part way under the car, near the wheel to be removed, but out of the way of the jack (this is a safety measure). Raise the jack until the wheel is an inch or two off the ground.

5 Remove the wheel bolts/nuts, and lift off the wheel. Drag out the spare wheel and slide the removed wheel under the car in its place.

6 Fit the spare wheel, then refit the bolts/nuts, and tighten them until they're just holding the wheel firmly. Remove the wheel from under the car, then lower the jack, and remove it from under the car.

7 Tighten one wheel bolt/nut securely, using the wheelbrace, then tighten the one diagonally opposite. Tighten the other two bolts/nuts in the same way, then refit the wheel trim, where applicable.

IN AN EMERGENCY

8 When you've finished, stow the removed wheel and the tools back in their correct locations. Check the pressure in the "new" tyre, with your gauge or at the next available garage. It's important to get the flat tyre repaired or renewed as soon as possible – don't put it off!

Space-saver spare tyres

These tyres are narrower than normal tyres, and are often inflated to a different pressure. There are usually speed and mileage restrictions marked on the tyre, or printed in the car handbook – make sure you observe these restrictions.
If you fit a "space-saver" tyre, have the flat tyre repaired and refitted as soon as possible.

The first priority must be safety. This might seem obvious, but it's easy to overlook certain points which could make the situation worse – always try to think clearly, and don't panic!

WHAT TO DO AT THE SCENE OF AN ACCIDENT

1. Further collisions and fire are the main dangers in a road accident.
   - If possible, warn other traffic.
   - Switch on the car's hazard warning flashers.
   - Set up a warning triangle a reasonable distance away from the accident to warn approaching drivers. Decide from which direction the approaching traffic will have least warning, and position the triangle accordingly.
   - Send someone to warn approaching traffic of the danger, and signal the traffic to slow down.
   - Switch off the ignition and make sure no-one smokes. This will reduce the possibility of a fire if there is a petrol leak.

2. Administer first aid if you've been properly trained.

IN AN EMERGENCY

3. Send someone to call the emergency services, and make sure that all the necessary information is given to the operator. Give the exact location of the accident, the number of vehicles and, if applicable, the number of casualties involved.
   - Call an ambulance if anyone is seriously injured or trapped.
   - Call the fire brigade if you think there is a risk of fire.
   - Call the police if any of the above conditions apply. In most cases, the accident must be reported to the police within 24 hours.

4. If you're involved in the accident, provide your personal and vehicle details to anyone having reasonable grounds to ask for them.

What the law says you must do if you have an accident
If you're involved in an accident which causes damage or injury to any other person, another vehicle, an animal, or roadside property.
1. Stop.
2. Give your own and the vehicle owner's name and address, the registration number of the vehicle, and your insurance details to anyone having reasonable grounds for requiring them.
3. If you don't give your name and address to any such person at the time, report the accident to the police as soon as possible, and in any case within 24 hours.

ACCIDENT
REPORT FORM

Use these pages to record all the relevant details in the event of an accident. You should transfer all the information recorded on this page onto the Motor Vehicle Accident Report form which you can obtain from your insurance company.

Other vehicle details

Driver
Full name ....
Address ....
....
....
Telephone number ....
Learner? ....

Owner (if different)
Full name ....
Address ....
....
....
Telephone number ....

Vehicle
Make ....
Model ....
Registration number ....

Insurance
Company ....
Type of cover ....
Policy number (if known) ....

Circumstances of accident

General
Date ....
Time ....
Place ....
Weather conditions ....
Approximate speed ....
Were the police called? ....
Details of station/officers attending ....
Did anyone sustain injury? ....

Witnesses
1 Full name ....
Address ....
....
....
Telephone number ....
2 Full name ....
Address ....
....
....
Telephone number ....

What happened?
Record all details of the incident. Include:
- The state of the road
- Whether all people involved were wearing seat belts
- If the accident was at night, were the streetlights on and were all vehicles' lights working?

Essential details to record

The following details will help you fill in an accident report form for your insurance company, and will help if the police become involved (see "Accident report form"). Inform your insurance company if you're involved in an accident, even if you're not going to make a claim.

1. The name and address of the other driver, and those of the vehicle owner, if different.
2. The name(s) and address(es) of any witness(es). Independent witnesses are especially important.
3. A description of any injury to yourself or anyone else
4. Details of any damage.
5. The other driver's insurance company details.
6. The registration number of the other vehicle.
7. The number of any police officer attending the scene.
8. The location, time and date of the accident.
9. The speed of the vehicles involved.
10. The width of the road, details of road signs, the state of the road, and the weather.
11. Any relevant marks or debris on the road.
12. A rough sketch of the accident.
13. Whether the vehicle occupants were wearing seat belts.
14. If it happened at night or in bad weather, whether vehicle lights or street lights were on.
15. If you have a camera, take pictures.
16. If the other driver refuses to give you their name and address, or if you think that they have committed a criminal offence, inform the police immediately.

WHAT TO DO IF YOUR CAR HAS BEEN STOLEN

If you left the car in a car park, are you sure that you've returned to where you left it? This might sound obvious, but large car parks, especially multi-storeys, can be pretty confusing!

The first thing to do if your car has been stolen is to contact the police, giving them the following information:

- Your name and address
- The make, colour and registration number of your car
- The location of your car
- The time that you left your car, and the time that you returned
- Details of any important or valuable items left in the car

After informing the police, contact your insurance company, and give them the details that you provided to the police – you'll have to fill in a claim form later, but you should inform your insurance company by phone as soon as possible after the incident. Most insurance companies provide a "help-line" - they will often arrange for you to be transported home, as will most of the motoring assistance organisations, if you're a member.

INFORM THE POLICE 999/112

WHAT TO DO IF YOUR CAR HAS BEEN BROKEN INTO

Check to see if anything has been stolen, and write down the details of any stolen items. Next, check your car for damage – is there any damage which will stop you from driving the car (wiring, ignition switch, steering, etc), which may not be obvious at first?

Once you've checked your car, contact the police, and give them the following information:
• Your name and address
• The make, colour and registration number of your car
• The location of your car
• The time that you left your car, and the time that you returned
• Details of any damage, and details of any items stolen

After informing the police, contact your insurance company, and give them the details that you provided to the police – you'll have to fill in a claim form later, but you should inform your insurance company by phone as soon as possible after the incident. Most insurance companies provide a "help-line" – if your car can't be driven, they will often arrange for recovery of your car, as will most of the motoring organisations, if you're a member.

WHAT TO DO IF YOU FILL UP WITH THE WRONG FUEL

Unleaded instead of leaded petrol

If you've just put a few litres of unleaded petrol in the tank, stop filling with unleaded, move to the leaded pump, and carry on filling with leaded petrol. You won't have any problems.

If you've filled the tank with unleaded petrol, drive the car until the fuel tank is about half empty, then fill the tank again with leaded petrol.

Diesel instead of petrol

Don't try to start the engine – if you do, it won't run for long, and you'll need to have all the fuel system components thoroughly cleaned and checked!

You'll need to have the fuel tank drained, cleaned and refilled with petrol before you can drive the car – call for help.

Petrol instead of diesel

If you've just put a few litres of petrol in the tank, stop filling with petrol, move to the diesel pump, and carry on filling with diesel. You won't have any problems.

If you've filled the tank with petrol, don't try to start the engine – if you do, it won't run for long, and you'll need to have all the fuel system components thoroughly cleaned and checked, which could be expensive!

You'll need to have the fuel tank drained, cleaned and refilled with diesel before you can drive the car – call for help.

DON'T
keep on trying to start the engine, hoping to pick up the last drops of fuel from the tank – you'll suck air and possibly dirt from the empty tank into the fuel system, which will make starting even harder when you've filled up!

WHAT TO DO IF YOU RUN OUT OF FUEL

If you have a can of fuel, switch off the ignition (NO SMOKING!) and empty it into the tank. Operate the starter for about 10 seconds several times, and if the engine now starts, fill the tank at a filling station. If the engine still won't start, dirt or air drawn into the fuel system could be causing problems, in which case you'll probably need professional help.

If you're out in the middle of nowhere, or on a motorway, all's not lost! On a motorway, you can use the emergency telephones to call for help, and if you're a member of one of the motoring organisations, they'll deliver an emergency can of fuel to you.

So why did you run out of fuel? If the fuel gauge indicated plenty of fuel in the tank, have the gauge checked, it's probably faulty. If there's a fuel leak, you should be able to smell the petrol vapour – DON'T drive the car until the problem is fixed!

Diesel engine cars

The engine may be difficult to start even when you've refilled the tank. This is due to air being drawn into the fuel lines when the fuel ran out. Most cars are fitted with a hand priming pump (refer to your car's handbook) in the fuel system to get the engine started. Normally, the pump takes the form of a large pushbutton on top of the fuel filter, or a rubber bulb in one of the fuel lines. Switch on the ignition, then pump the priming button or bulb until you feel resistance (this could take more than thirty presses), indicating that the air has been expelled. Try to start the engine with the accelerator fully depressed – the engine should eventually start. If the engine still won't start, air has probably been drawn into the fuel injection pump – fuel lines must be disconnected, so professional help is needed.

IN AN EMERGENCY

WHAT TO DO IF YOUR WINDSCREEN BREAKS

Most cars have "laminated" windscreens. If a laminated windscreen is hit, it may chip or crack, but it should still be possible to see through it clearly, and the glass shouldn't shatter. On older cars without laminated windscreens, the glass is more likely to break or shatter.

Small chips and cracks can often be repaired. If a crack develops, have it repaired as soon as possible (a large crack will mean a new windscreen).

If you can't see clearly, or if the glass shatters, stop in a safe place, and switch on your hazard warning lights. Never try to knock the glass out – you may cut yourself. Don't drive with no windscreen – it will be extremely windy, and you risk being hit by loose glass particles, insects, and road debris.

Windscreen Repair
There are several emergency mobile windscreen repair companies, who will come to your assistance at the roadside if necessary – it's worth keeping the phone number of one of these companies with you. In any case, your insurance company will usually pay for windscreen repair if you pay a small excess.

WHAT TO DO IF THE ENGINE OVERHEATS

Cars most often overheat when stuck in traffic – keep an eye on the temperature gauge. Overheating can cause serious and expensive engine damage, so watch for the warning signs!

Place a large wad of rag over the coolant filler cap, and release the cap very slowly to allow the pressure to escape – there is a risk of scalding from steam and hot coolant!

What causes overheating?

Apart from simply getting too hot on a summer's day in traffic, here are the most common causes of engine overheating:

- Low coolant level
- Faulty cooling fan
- Leakage
- Faulty coolant pump
- Broken coolant pump drivebelt (where applicable)

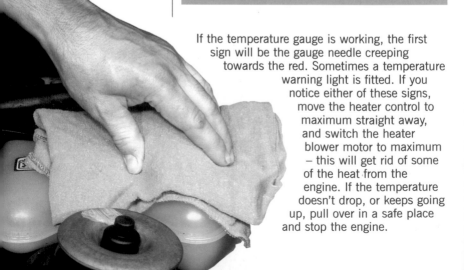

If the temperature gauge is working, the first sign will be the gauge needle creeping towards the red. Sometimes a temperature warning light is fitted. If you notice either of these signs, move the heater control to maximum straight away, and switch the heater blower motor to maximum – this will get rid of some of the heat from the engine. If the temperature doesn't drop, or keeps going up, pull over in a safe place and stop the engine.

IN AN EMERGENCY

If the level is low, it's time to top up (see "Coolant level check"). You can use plain water in an emergency. If almost all the coolant has been lost, don't fill the system with cold water whilst the engine is hot, as this might cause engine damage.

In extreme cases, the first sign of overheating may be steam coming from under the bonnet. Pull over and stop as soon as possible. Don't open the bonnet until the steam stops.

If no steam is coming from under the bonnet, open the bonnet to help the heat escape, and wait for the engine to cool down!

A very hot engine takes time to cool, and you'll have to wait at least half-an-hour before the temperature drops to normal.

Check under the car for coolant leakage – coolant is usually brightly coloured (often green, yellow or pink), and will probably be steaming if it's hot! If there's a leak, call for assistance (see "What to do if you break down").

When the engine has cooled, check the coolant level (see "Coolant level check") – if there's been no leakage, and no steam, the level will probably be above the "maximum" mark (hot coolant expands). If the coolant level is OK, and there's no leakage, it's safe to carry on driving, but keep an eye on the temperature gauge!

HOW TO TOW A CAR

Special towing eyes are normally provided at the front and rear of the car. Sometimes the towing eyes may be hidden under covers, and some cars have screw-in towing eyes provided in the tool kit – check your car's handbook for details.

Obviously you'll need a suitable tow-rope. It's worth carrying one just in case you ever need it. If you've never towed before, take note of the following points:

- When being towed - the ignition key must be turned to the "on" position so that the steering lock is released. This will also allow the indicators, horn and brake lights to work. If the battery is flat or there's some other electrical problem, you'll have to use hand signals.

- If you're driving a car that's being towed – the brake servo won't work (because the engine isn't running). This means that you'll have to press the brake pedal harder than usual, so allow for longer braking distances. Also, power steering (where applicable) won't work when the engine isn't running, so you'll need more effort to turn the steering wheel. If the breakdown doesn't stop the engine running, you could allow it to idle so that the brake servo and power steering work normally. On Citroën models with hydraulic suspension (BX, CX, XM, etc), if the engine is not running the brakes won't work.

IN AN EMERGENCY

- If the car being towed has automatic transmission - the gear lever should be moved to the "N" position. Often, the manufacturer recommends that you don't exceed a certain speed or distance - check your car's handbook for details. Ideally, a car with automatic transmission should be towed with the driven wheels off the ground.

- An "On tow" notice should be displayed at the rear of the car on tow.

- Make sure that both drivers know details of the route to be taken before moving off.

- Before moving away - the tow car should be driven slowly forwards to take up any slack in the tow rope.

- The driver of the car on tow should try to keep the tow rope tight at all times – by gently using the brakes if necessary.

- Drive smoothly at all times – especially when moving away from a standstill.

- Allow plenty of time to slow down and stop – especially when approaching junctions and traffic queues.

WARNING
Take care not to burn yourself on a hot exhaust!

PROBLEMS WITH THE EXHAUST

The exhaust doesn't last forever, and you'll have to have part of the system renewed if you keep the car for a few years. There are a number of exhaust specialists who carry out work, with a guarantee, at far cheaper rates than a dealer.

Exhaust hangs down or falls off

If the exhaust rattles or hits the road, it's usually due to a broken mounting. You can carry out a temporary repair using a piece of stout wire.
If the exhaust has broken, you may still be able to support the broken section with wire.
If the exhaust has sheared off completely, you're going to have a noisy drive to the nearest exhaust repair centre!

Exhaust blowing?

A "blowing" exhaust can usually be heard when accelerating or decelerating. It's annoying, and also means hot gases are escaping from the exhaust – this can damage surrounding components, and is dangerous if the fumes get inside the car (exhaust gases are poisonous).
The exhaust may blow due to a leaking joint, or because there's a hole in the system.
Temporary repairs can be done using exhaust repair putty, or a repair bandage (follow the instructions supplied), but if there's a hole, the best answer is to have a new exhaust section fitted.

BUYING JUMP LEADS

- Make sure that the leads are thick enough for the job. Some poor-quality leads have very thin wires, and they can melt or catch fire when you use them.
- Make sure that the leads are long enough!
- The leads should be colour coded: red for positive, and black for negative.
- Make sure that the leads have good-quality clamps which will grip securely.
- Are the leads flexible when they're cold? Some go almost rigid and become very difficult to connect.
- Try to buy leads with a case to stop them getting tangled up and keep them in good condition when not being used.

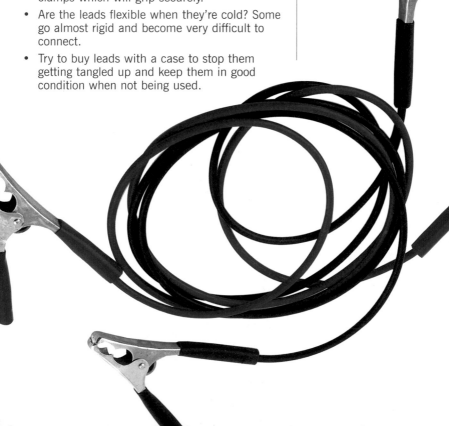

HOW TO USE JUMP LEADS

If you have a flat battery, you can start the car by using jump leads to connect its battery temporarily to a charged one, whether in or out of another vehicle.

1 Position the vehicles so that the batteries are close, but don't let the vehicles touch. Switch off the ignition and all electrical equipment on both vehicles, apply the handbrakes, and ensure the gears are in neutral (manual) or "P" (automatic).

2 Connect one end of the RED jump lead to the POSITIVE (+) terminal of the flat battery. Don't let the other end of the red lead touch any vehicle metal.

3 Connect the other end of the RED lead to the POSITIVE (+) terminal of the boosting battery.

4 Connect one end of the BLACK jump lead to the NEGATIVE (–) terminal of the boosting battery.

5 Connect the other end of the BLACK lead to a bolt or metal bracket, well away from the battery, on the engine block of the vehicle to be started.

6 Ensure that the jump leads cannot come into contact with any moving parts of either engine. Start the engine of the boosting vehicle and run it at a fast idle. Now start the engine of the stranded vehicle and ensure that it's running properly.

7 Stop the engine of the boosting vehicle ONLY, then disconnect the jump leads in the reverse order of connection.

8 Keep the use of electrical equipment to a minimum, and remember that it will take some time for the alternator to charge the battery. Don't stop the engine again too soon – and try not to stall it whilst driving.

WHAT TO DO IF YOUR CAR WON'T START

There aren't many things more frustrating than an engine that won't start - but try to think logically. If you're at home, it's better than being stranded miles from anywhere. If you're a member of one of the motoring organisations, and your membership includes "home-start", now's the time to pick up the phone. If not, run through the following checks.

1 Immobiliser - check that you know how this works, and make sure that you know the starting procedure, otherwise it may seem like you have a "dead" engine.

2 Automatic transmission – the engine won't start unless the selector lever is in the "N" or "P" position. This is a safety feature, and is not a fault.

IN AN EMERGENCY

3 If there's no familiar starter motor sound (or just a clicking noise), then the starter motor may be faulty, or the battery may be flat (see "Batteries").

4 You could be out of fuel (faulty gauges have been known, so don't rely totally on the reading). Consider whether this is a possibility (not if you've just filled up!). See "What to do if you run out of fuel".

5 On some petrol engine cars, there's a cut-off switch which stops the fuel flow in the event of an accident. Sometimes, the switch can be triggered by a pot hole or minor bump – you'll have to reset it manually. Check your car's handbook for details, and try resetting it. Most switches can be reset by pushing a button on the top of the switch.

6 Check for damp ignition leads (try a water-dispersant spray), or worn spark plugs on petrol engines. Other possibilities are air or water in the fuel system (diesel engines), a blocked fuel system, a badly worn engine, or a serious fault – professional help is probably needed at this stage.

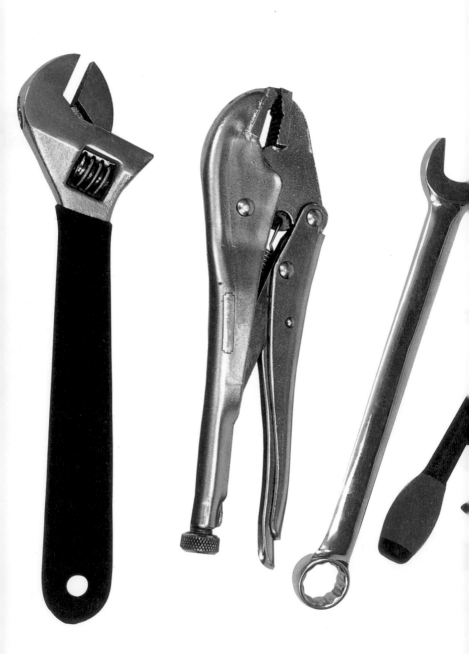

TOOLS

A selection of basic tools is essential if you're thinking of maintaining your own car. The tool kit supplied with most cars won't allow you to do much more than change a wheel!
Even if you're not going to carry out any maintenance, it's a good idea to carry a few extra tools just in case –
if you can't fix a problem yourself, someone else might be able to help if you can supply a screwdriver.
You don't need to buy the most expensive tools, but generally you get what you pay for, and a good quality set of tools will last for many years.

WHAT DO I NEED?

The tools in "Things you should always carry" are what you'll need if you're not planning to do any DIY maintenance.
If you are going to carry out your own basic maintenance, there are a few extra tools you'll need.

A toolbox to keep everything together

Self-locking grips

A wad of clean cloth

Spanners, or basic socket set (covering range 8 to 26mm)

Torch

Screwdrivers (flat-blade and crosshead)

Once you've built up a reasonable tool kit, you need to keep the tools in good condition. Never leave tools lying around after they've been used.

Take care when using tools, and don't try to use them for a job they're not designed for.

TOOLS

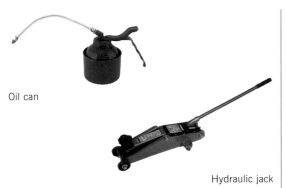

Oil can

Hydraulic jack

- A comprehensive socket set (8 to 26 mm)
- Oil filter removal tool
- Sump drain plug tool
- Oil can
- Funnel
- Oil draining container
- Self-locking grips
- Scriber
- Mains-powered light, with extension lead
- Hydraulic jack
- Axle stands
- Brake bleed nipple spanner
- Brake bleeding kit
- Soft-faced mallet
- Ball pein hammer
- Torque wrench
- Tyre pump
- Small wire brush
- Junior hacksaw
- Fine emery cloth
- Electric drill – with a good range of twist drills
- Overalls
- Old newspapers and clean rags for cleaning and mopping up

Generally there are safety standards for tools. Usually the packaging, or the tools themselves, will show that they meet a particular standard. You can buy plenty of tools which don't meet any standards, but they're more likely to let you down, and they're unlikely to last as long.

You don't have to buy the most expensive tools, but it's a good idea to steer clear of the very cheap ones.

You'll have to make sensible compromises when choosing tools. If you're on a limited budget, it's best to spend a little more on the tools you're likely to use most often – for instance a good set of spanners should last you a lifetime, whereas a poor quality set will tend to wear, and won't fit properly. Combination spanners (ring one end, open-ended the other) are the best buy if you can afford them, as they give the advantages of both types of spanner.

If you find that you need a special tool which it isn't economic to buy, you may be able to borrow or hire it from a local garage or a tool hire specialist for a reasonable charge.

SIMPLE CHECKS AND SERVICING

The following pages show you how to perform some checks and simple renewal procedures on your car. They are not particularly difficult or dirty tasks, and will help to ensure your car's reliability and safety. They can also save you money by helping you spot a minor problem before it becomes serious.

If you're new to car care, probably the worst way to start is to try and do everything straight away – even assuming that you want to. If you're keen to acquire more background knowledge on how your car works, then a vehicle maintenance course, such as those run by adult education colleges, will provide useful insight into the whys and wherefores.

This book will help you work out what may be wrong, and have a reasonably informed conversation with a mechanic about your car.

Whatever your level of knowledge or commitment, we suggest you use this chapter as a gradual introduction to the tasks and routines involved in keeping your car in good shape, and that you undertake just as much, or as little, as you feel happy to do yourself.

ALL ABOUT OIL

Why does the engine need oil?

Oil lubricates, cleans and cools the moving parts of the engine. It also helps to prevent corrosion and the build-up of sludge deposits, and can have an important effect on cold starting and fuel economy.

Without oil, the engine would very quickly seize up. The oil provides a film between the moving parts - without it, friction from metal-to-metal contact would soon cause severe overheating, rapidly wrecking the engine.

Engine oil deteriorates with use, which is why it needs changing periodically. In between changes it is important to keep it topped up to the correct level.

The engine oil and filter should be renewed at the manufacturer's recommended intervals (normally at least every 6,000 miles or 12 months).

Why do I need to check the oil?

Checking the engine oil regularly is one of the most important things you can do to keep the car running smoothly. Even a healthy engine may consume a little oil, so you'll almost certainly need to top up the oil once or twice between changes. It's a good idea to keep a top-up pack of oil in the car for this purpose.

How often you need to check the oil will depend on your car and the sort of driving you do. Once a week is often suggested, which is probably erring on the side of safety for most drivers. Once a month is better than not at all!

The red oil warning light on the instrument panel is to warn that the engine oil pressure is dangerously low (due to a serious leak, very low oil level, or engine wear) – it is not an oil level

warning light. It should light up when you first switch on the ignition, then go out and stay out as soon as the engine starts. If the oil pressure warning light comes on when the engine is running, stop immediately.

What sort of oil do I need?

Most oils may look very similar, but there are different types and grades varying widely in performance, so it's important that the oil you use meets (or better, exceeds) the specification laid down by the car manufacturer. Additives in the oil play an important rôle in determining its performance; cheap oils may have an inferior additive package or even none at all. It pays, therefore, to choose an oil with a reputable name. We recommend Duckhams oils.

There are two main things to look out for in the oil specification - the viscosity (thickness) shown by the "SAE" rating, and the quality (indicated by the "API" or "ACEA" rating). These specifications will be marked on the oil packaging. If the packaging doesn't have any specifications marked on it, or if there's no "API" or "ACEA" rating, don't buy it! The cheapest oils are usually "mineral-based", the mid-price oils "semi-synthetic" and the most expensive oils "fully-synthetic". Obviously it is a waste of money to put fully-synthetic oil into an old banger, but it is also certainly false economy to use a lower quality of oil than that specified by the car manufacturer.

Technical Information

SAE 15W/40
Mineral formula
Oil Colour: Green

Meets requirements of:
API SG/SH/SJ,CCMC
G4, ACEA A3-96

Further Information

If you would like any further information on oil, visit Duckhams at **www.duckhams.co.uk**. Alternatively you can call the Duckhams Consumer Helpline on 0800 212 988 or e-mail your questions to **ducktech@bp.com**.

OIL LEVEL CHECK

You will need a wad of clean cloth, a pack of engine oil of the correct type (if you need to top up), and a funnel.

Before you start, park the car on level ground and make sure the engine has been stopped for at least five minutes.

1 Find the dipstick, and pull it right out of its tube. The top of the dipstick is often brightly coloured to help you find it.

2 Wipe the oil off the dipstick using a clean cloth, and look for the oil level marks on the end of the dipstick.

3 Push the dipstick slowly all the way back into its tube, then pull it out again. The level should be between the upper and lower marks.

SIMPLE CHECKS AND SERVICING

4 If the level is near the lower mark, you need to top up. To top up, find the oil filler cap on top of the engine. There may also be filler caps for other systems, so if you're not sure, look in your car's handbook.

5 Remove the filler cap (some caps unscrew, while others are a push-fit), and pour in a little oil. Don't overfill the engine – it can cause leaks, and possibly damage.

6 Wait a few seconds for the oil to drain down to the bottom of the engine, then re-check the oil level. If you need to, repeat the topping up and checking procedure until the oil level reaches the upper mark on the dipstick. When you've finished, refit the filler cap tightly, wipe away any spills, and make sure that the dipstick is pushed all the way into its tube.

The coolant reservoir may be transparent, or it may have a level indicator inside, which is visible once the cap has been removed.

COOLANT LEVEL CHECK

The coolant is pumped around the engine, and cools it by means of the radiator. If the level gets too low, it could cause overheating and serious engine damage. It's normal to have to top up occasionally, but the need for regular topping-up suggests that there's a leak or some other problem which should be fixed before it gets serious. Make sure you use the right type of coolant for topping up – some cars use coolant which cannot be mixed with other types (check in your car's handbook for details).

Check the level once a week, or before a long journey. The coolant should be renewed at the manufacturer's recommended intervals. A few manufacturers use "lifetime" coolant, which is designed to last the life of the car – check in your car's handbook for details.

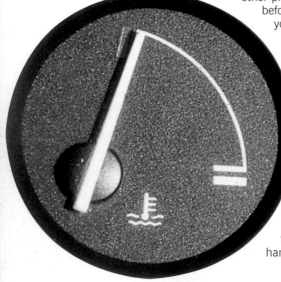

1 Check the level is up to the relevant mark (or between the "MIN" and "MAX" marks). If you need to remove the reservoir cap, carefully unscrew the cap and check the level.

2 If the level's low, top up using a 50/50 mixture of water and antifreeze (or clean tap water in an emergency) to bring the level up to the appropriate mark. Don't overfill.

WARNING
Never undo the reservoir cap while the engine is hot – danger of scalding. Unscrew the cap slowly and allow any pressure to escape. Wash off any accidental splashes from the skin, and from the car's bodywork – it can cause paint damage.

3 Refit the cap tightly afterwards, and wipe away any spillage.

BRAKE FLUID LEVEL CHECK

If the brake fluid level gets too low, the brakes will work poorly, or not at all. Regular checking of the fluid level will warn you if a leak's developing. The fluid level falls gradually as the brake pads and shoes wear, but if you're topping-up regularly, there must be a leak – stop driving the car until the leak's been found and fixed.

Check the brake fluid level once a week, or before a long journey.

The fluid should be renewed every 12 months, regardless of mileage.

Note: Some Citroën cars do not use the same type of fluid – see "LHM fluid level check (certain Citroën cars)".

1 Make sure the car is level, then wipe the brake fluid reservoir clean. The level must be kept between the "MAX" and "MIN" marks.

SIMPLE CHECKS AND SERVICING

2 If topping-up is needed, unscrew and remove the reservoir cap. Usually, the inside of the cap fits down into the fluid, so pull it out slowly, and place it on a piece of clean cloth to catch drips.

3 Top up to the "MAX" mark. Use a good quality brake fluid which meets the standard DOT 4 (this will be marked on the container). Always use new fluid from a freshly-opened container.

4 Refit the reservoir cap and discard the cloth.

WARNING
The fluid used in Citroën hydraulic systems is LHM mineral fluid, which is green in colour. The use of any other type of fluid, including normal brake fluid, will damage the system rubber seals and hoses. Keep the LHM fluid sealed in its original container. Note that most Citroën cars with conventional suspension (springs and shock absorbers instead of hydraulics) use conventional brake hydraulic fluid in the braking system, and automatic transmission fluid in the power steering system – don't use LHM fluid in these systems.

LHM FLUID LEVEL CHECK (certain Citroën cars)

Certain Citroën cars use a hydraulic system to control the suspension, brakes and power steering. This system uses a special hydraulic fluid (LHM). As with any hydraulic system, a need for frequent topping-up can only be due to a leak, which should be found and fixed without delay.
The LHM fluid level should be checked every week, or before a long journey, and the fluid should be renewed every 36,000 miles. Renewing the fluid can be a tricky job, and it's best to get it done by a suitably-equipped garage.

To check the LHM hydraulic fluid level, first start the engine, and with the engine idling, set the suspension height control lever inside the car to the "Maximum" position.

SIMPLE CHECKS AND SERVICING

1 The fluid level is indicated by a sight glass on top of the fluid reservoir in the engine compartment. The level indicator float should be between the two rings on the sight glass – the level indication is only accurate when the car has stabilised at its maximum height.

2 If you need to top up, use clean LHM fluid. Remove the filler cap on top of the fluid reservoir, and top up until the level indicator float is between the two rings. When the level's correct, refit the reservoir cap, and stop the engine.

CLUTCH FLUID LEVEL CHECK

Some cars with manual transmission have a hydraulic clutch. Sometimes, the clutch hydraulic system may be sealed, or may share a common reservoir with the braking system – alternatively, there may be a separate clutch fluid reservoir (check your car's handbook for details). If the fluid needs topping-up, there must be a leak – a bad leak will stop the clutch working, so have the system checked if you need to top up regularly. Check the clutch fluid level once a week, or before a long journey.

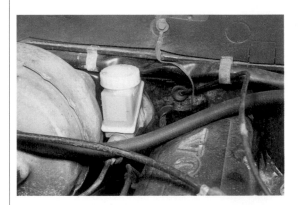

1 Make sure the car's parked on level ground, then wipe the clutch fluid reservoir clean if it's dirty. The fluid level must always be kept between the "MAX" and "MIN" marks – if there are no level markings, the fluid level should normally be up to the lower edge of the reservoir filler neck.

2 If topping-up is needed, unscrew and remove the reservoir cap.

3 Top up using new brake fluid. Use a good quality brake fluid which meets the standard DOT 4 (this will be marked on the container). Always use new fluid from a freshly-opened container - using old brake fluid could result in the clutch not working properly.

4 Refit the reservoir cap when you've finished.

POWER STEERING FLUID LEVEL CHECK

If your car has power steering and the fluid level's low, there may be a hissing or squealing sound as the steering wheel is turned. If the level is very low, or the system's leaking, the power steering system may be damaged, and the steering wheel will be harder to turn.

Most power steering systems use automatic transmission fluid, but you should always check with your car's handbook – different types of system use different fluids, and you could cause damage if you use the wrong fluid. Have the system checked for leaks if you need to top up regularly.

Check the power steering fluid level once a week, or before a long journey.

1 If you need to remove the filler cap to check the level, wipe around the cap first, then unscrew the cap.

SIMPLE CHECKS AND SERVICING

2 Read off the fluid level, and top up if necessary. Sometimes there may be "HOT" and "COLD" level markings for use depending on whether the engine's hot or cold – the level should be up to the relevant mark.

3 If the level's low, wipe around the filler cap, then remove it, if not already done, and top up to the correct mark. Don't overfill. Refit the filler cap tightly afterwards.

The power steering fluid reservoir may be transparent with level markings on the outside, or it may have a level dipstick fitted to the filler cap.

TYRE CHECKS

The importance of tyres is often overlooked, the only contact with the road is through the tyres. They must be free from damage, correctly inflated, and must have enough tread to give the necessary grip. Check the correct pressures with your car's handbook. Note that pressures should be checked when the tyres are cold (not driven for at least 30 minutes), and that the pressures may be different for front and rear tyres, and also for fully loaded conditions. The pressure marked on the side of the tyre is the maximum, not the running pressure.

Taking each wheel in turn, unscrew the valve dust cap and put it somewhere safe.

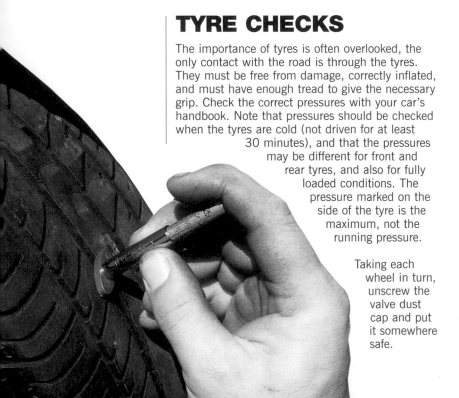

SIMPLE CHECKS AND SERVICING

Check the tyre pressure by pushing the nozzle of the gauge firmly on to the valve so that no air can be heard escaping. Remove the gauge from the valve and check the reading.

If the pressure needs increasing slightly, you can drive to the nearest garage, or use your pump according to the instructions.

Check the pressure again. If it's now too high, gently press the pin in the centre of the tyre valve to release a small quantity of air at a time. Re-check the pressure with the gauge. Refit the dust cap when you've finished.

Don't forget the spare tyre just because it's out of sight. Inflate this to the highest of the pressures quoted for your car.

All tyres must have at least the minimum legal amount of tread - that's 1.6 mm in the UK, although in practice it's better to change tyres well before they become this worn. Use a tread depth gauge according to the instructions to check the tread remaining.

Ideally you should also check the general condition of each tyre. You'll need to jack up each wheel in turn and rotate it. Look for any damage, bulges, or foreign bodies in treads or sidewalls, and for uneven tread wear, indicating possible wheel misalignment. If you find any of these, drive carefully to the tyre specialist for further advice.

Tyre pumps

There are two basic types of pump: foot pumps and electric pumps.

The easiest type of pump to use is an electric one, with a built-in gauge, that plugs into the car's cigarette lighter.

Foot pumps come in various shapes and sizes, and basically you get what you pay for. If you can afford it, it's best to buy a pump with a metal barrel because it will be more robust. Bear in mind that the bigger the pump, the easier it will be to blow up a tyre!

SIMPLE CHECKS AND SERVICING

Tyre pressure gauges

Pressure gauges come in various patterns: plunger-types, dial gauges, and electronic (digital) gauges. Which one you choose is really down to personal preference, but the easiest type of gauge to use is a dial-type.
High quality, high accuracy gauges can be expensive, but you don't need to spend a fortune. As long as your gauge is reasonably accurate and robust, it should serve you well. Note that even if the pump you're using has a built-in pressure gauge, it's always best to check the pressure with a separate gauge. The gauges built into pumps can be inaccurate, and are easily damaged when using the pump. Likewise, the gauges attached to garage air lines are notoriously inaccurate. By all means use the air line to inflate your tyres, but use your own gauge to check the pressure afterwards.

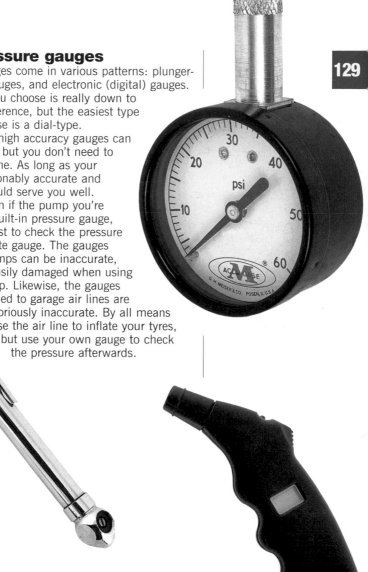

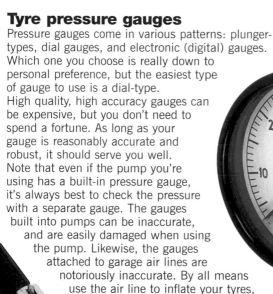

WARNING
Never use engine
antifreeze in the
washer system – it's
not only hazardous to
health, but it will also
damage the car's
paintwork and trim.
Use a good quality
screenwash
additive/de-icer.

SCREENWASH FLUID LEVEL CHECK

You can use plain water in the washer reservoir,
but using a good quality screenwash additive will
help clean the screen, and its anti-icing properties
are essential in winter to stop the washer jets
freezing up. Note the directions on the container
as to the quantity to add.

Check the screenwash fluid level once a week, or
before a long journey. Many people find it
convenient to top up the screenwash fluid when
they fill up with fuel.

The windscreen washer reservoir is usually located
in the engine compartment. If your car is fitted
with headlight washers, the headlight washers
normally use fluid from the windscreen washer
fluid reservoir, although on some cars a separate
reservoir may be fitted. Similarly, if a tailgate
washer system is fitted, there may be a combined
windscreen/tailgate fluid reservoir, or there may be
a separate tailgate washer fluid reservoir
(sometimes in the boot).

SIMPLE CHECKS AND SERVICING

1 If you need to top up, wipe away any dirt from around the filler neck, then pull off the filler cap.

2 Fill the reservoir, then refit the cap firmly, and wipe away any spillage. A funnel can make it easier to top up.

3 You can clear a blocked washer jet by poking the fine nozzle gently with a pin. You can also use the pin to swivel the "eyeball" so that the jet is aimed correctly – but don't break the pin off in the nozzle.

WINDSCREEN WIPER CHECK AND RENEWAL

It's a good idea to check the wiper blades regularly for damage and wear. Correctly working windscreen wipers are an important safety item as well as a legal requirement. If they tend to smear, or fail to clear water from the screen, the wiper blades probably need to be renewed.

Fitting a new wiper blade

1 With the ignition off, lift the wiper arm until it locks in the upright position. If the arm won't lock in position, hold it until you can remove the blade; take care not to allow the arm to spring back.

2 To remove the blade, first turn it at right-angles to the arm. Press the securing tab(s), where fitted, then slide the blade out of the hooked end of the arm.

3 Fit the adapter to the new blade (look on the packet for details).

4 Fit the blade to the arm, making sure that it's fully home. Lower the arm gently onto the screen. Check that the wipers work before driving the car.

Looking after your wiper blades

- Carefully lift the wiper arm from the windscreen (take care not to allow it to spring back against the glass), then wipe the cleaning edge of the blade with a clean cloth dipped in screenwash concentrate. Check the blade rubber carefully for damage. If you find cracks or tears, renew the blade.

- When laying the blade back in position on the glass, make sure that it's pushing on the glass correctly. If the blade pushes on the glass too hard, it will squeak and may cause smearing, and if the blade doesn't push hard enough, it won't clear the glass effectively. This sort of problem is normally cured by fitting new wiper arms.

- If the blades don't wipe the screen properly, renew them, even if they look OK. It's a good idea to renew the wiper blades once a year in any case, preferably before the start of winter.

- When using the wipers to clear the screen, always make sure that the screen is wet. Don't use a higher wiper speed than you need when it's raining, and if your car has separate switches for the washers and wipers, always make sure that you operate the washers to wet the screen before switching on the wiper.

- In winter, if you switch on the wipers with the blades frozen in place, you can quickly burn out the wiper motor, which could be an expensive mistake. Frozen wiper blades can usually be freed using de-icer – if you pull the blades from a frozen screen take care not to tear the rubbers.

If you're on a tight budget, it's possible to buy replacement rubbers only, but to fit these, you need to dismantle the blade, and this can be very fiddly. It's advisable to renew the whole blade because the springs and hinges weaken with age. You can buy new wiper blades from an authorised dealer for your car, or from most motor factors and car accessory shops. When you go to buy new blades, you'll need to know the make, model, and the year of manufacture of your car. As you remove the old wiper blade, note carefully how it's fitted, to help when fitting the new blade.

FUSE RENEWAL

Fuses protect a car's electrical circuits from being
overloaded. If an electrically-powered item stops
working, it could be that the fuse has blown. If you
replace a fuse and it blows again, there's almost
certainly a fault in the wiring or the item concerned.

How to change a fuse

Before you start, switch off the ignition and any
other electrical circuits.

1 Check your car's
handbook for where to find
the fuses. The fuses are
usually somewhere under a
dashboard cover, but some
(or all) might be located
under the bonnet.

2 To remove a fuse, simply
pull it from its panel. On
some cars you'll find a
plastic tool for removing
the fuses.

3 The new fuse must be
the same rating as the old
one. It should be the same
colour, or have the same
number stamped on it.

4 Push the new fuse firmly
into its slot in the fusebox.
Switch on the circuit
concerned. If the new fuse
blows, there's a problem.

Fuses keep blowing?

Fuses are designed to break an electrical circuit when a predetermined current is reached, in order to protect the component(s) and wiring. Any excessive current flow will be due to a fault in the circuit, usually a short-circuit.

A blown fuse can be recognised by the melted wire in the middle.

If a fuse keeps blowing, first of all, check that it's the correct rating for the circuit. Fuse locations and ratings may be marked on the fusebox or the cover, or may be given in your car's handbook. Fuses have standard colour codes. Refer to the markings on the fusebox cover for details of the circuits protected.

If the fuse is of the correct rating, and it still keeps blowing, have the circuit tested for faults.

LIGHTS AND

INDICATORS

Bulb check

You should check the bulbs regularly (once a week
and before a long journey). A faulty bulb can be
dangerous, and is also against the law. It's worthwhile carrying a spare set of bulbs in the car (in
some foreign countries this is a legal requirement).

136

1 With the ignition on, switch on the
sidelights, then walk around the car
to check that the front and rear lights
work. Repeat the check with dipped
and main beam headlights. Check
the rear foglights with the headlights
on dip and any front driving lights or
foglights at the same time.

2 Leave the ignition on, then operate
the direction indicators, and check
that all the bulbs are working. Don't
forget the side repeater lights. The
remaining lights will usually flash
faster than normal if a bulb has
blown.

3 Switch on the hazard warning
lights, and check that all the
indicator lights flash. Again, don't
forget the side repeater lights.

4 Still with the ignition on, push the
brake pedal, and check that both
brake lights work (also check the
high-level brake light if you have
one). Perform this check by reversing
up to a window or garage door and
looking for the reflection, or ask an
assistant to look for you. Switch off
the ignition when you've finished
checking.

SIMPLE CHECKS AND SERVICING

Fitting a new bulb

When buying a new bulb, you'll need to know what type of fitting (push-fit, bayonet-fit, festoon, etc), and what rating you need. Ratings are measured in watts (W), and are normally marked on the metal base, or on the glass itself. Some cars have combined tail/stop light bulbs. These bulbs are a bayonet-fit, with offset pins to ensure that the bulb is fitted the correct way round.

The halogen bulbs used in headlights and front foglights have an "H" number to identify their type. It's a good idea to carry a set of spare bulbs in your car, and it's compulsory in some countries.

Here's a general guide on how to change a halogen-type headlight bulb; you may find differences (for instance access, and bulb type) for your car. Before you start, make sure that the headlights are switched off. Remember that a bulb that has just failed or been switched off may be extremely hot.

1 Where necessary, unclip the cover from the rear of the headlight for access to the bulb.

2 Disconnect the wiring plug from the back of the bulb, and pull the rubber cover from the back of the bulb.

3 Release the spring clip, by squeezing its legs together and pulling the clip away from the bulbholder, then pull out the bulb.

4 Don't touch the glass on the new bulb with your fingers – hold it with a tissue or clean cloth. If you accidentally touch the bulb, clean it with a little methylated spirit.

5 Halogen bulbs usually have tangs around their edge so that they only fit in one position. Slide the new bulb into position, then secure it with the spring clip. Refit the bulb cover and reconnect the wiring plug, as applicable.

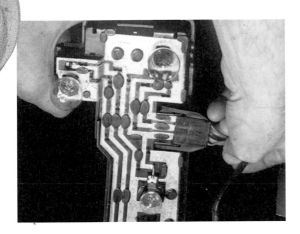

Faulty lights?

If you find that a light isn't working properly, and the bulb hasn't blown, the most likely cause is a bad electrical connection.

Corrosion
Check the wiring connector(s) for corrosion, and also check the contacts inside the bulbholder. Water may not be able to get in, but condensation can cause trouble.
Clean the affected area, then spray the components with water dispersant. You might have to replace the affected part(s).

Earth connections
If there's no trace of corrosion check the earth connection(s).
Usually the earth wire is bolted to a nearby body panel, or plugged into an earth connector block attached to the body. Check the connections are not corroded, and are tight. If a connection is bolted to a body panel, try cleaning the area of the bodywork with abrasive paper, then reconnect and spray it with water dispersant.

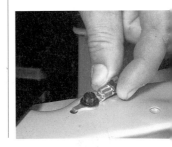

Indicators don't work?

Symptom	Possible cause	Action
Indicators flash faster on one side of the car	• Blown bulb • Incorrect (too low wattage) bulb fitted	• Fit a new bulb • Check the wattage of the bulbs
Indicators flash slower on one side of the car	• Poor earth connection in circuit • Incorrect bulb (too high wattage) bulb fitted	• Refer to "Faulty lights?" • Check the wattage of the bulbs
Indicators come on but don't flash	• Faulty flasher unit • Wiring fault	• Fit a new flasher unit • Have the circuit checked
Indicators don't come on at all	• Blown fuse • Faulty indicator switch • Faulty flasher unit • Wiring fault	• Fit a new fuse • Have the switch tested • Fit a new flasher unit • Have the circuit checked

AUXILIARY DRIVEBELTS

Auxiliary drivebelts are usually driven by a pulley on the end of the crankshaft and drive the engine ancillaries, such as the alternator, power steering and air conditioning compressor and, on some cars, the coolant pump. One drivebelt may drive all the ancillaries, or several separate drivebelts may be used.

On diesel-engined cars, the fuel injection pump may be driven by an auxiliary drivebelt, or by the engine timing belt - in either case, the belt will be enclosed, and normally won't need any regular attention (except for renewal at the recommended intervals). Drivebelt checking is part of the maintenance schedule on most cars, and you'll almost certainly have to renew the drivebelt(s) at some stage if you keep the car for any length of time.

Buying a spare auxiliary drivebelt
It's always best to carry the correct spare drivebelt for your particular car. You can buy replacement drivebelts from motor factors or car accessory shops, but you may find you have to go to an authorised dealer. To help find the correct new belt, if possible take the old belt along with you. Drivebelts stretch in use, so don't worry if a new belt is a few millimetres shorter than a used one.

141

Checking an auxiliary drivebelt

1 Most manufacturers specify a tension for each belt, but you should be able to tension a belt correctly by a little trial-and-error. The belt must be tight enough to stop slipping, but not so tight that it strains the ancillaries – if you can push the belt down by about 5 to 10 mm using light finger pressure at the middle of the longest belt run between the pulleys, this should be good enough for most engines.

2 It can be tricky to reach a drivebelt, and access may be easiest from under the car (you may have to unbolt covers for access). Check the whole length of the belt - you'll probably need to turn the engine. Usually, the easiest way to turn the engine is to use a spanner on the bolt or nut fitted to the pulley end of the crankshaft.

3 Look for cracks, splitting and fraying on the surface of the belt, and check for signs of shiny patches. If you find any damage or wear, a new belt should be fitted.

4 An automatic or a manually-adjustable tensioner may be fitted. A manually-adjustable belt may be adjusted by moving the ancillary it drives (such as the alternator), or there may be a separate adjuster assembly.

5 A belt will squeal if it's too slack, especially when pulling away from a standstill. A belt that's too tight may "hum".

Can I drive the car with a broken auxiliary drivebelt?

It's a good idea to carry a spare drivebelt in your car, in case you need it – even if you don't fit it yourself, you'll have the correct belt for someone else to fit for you. One belt may drive more than one accessory, so make sure you know exactly what was driven by the broken drivebelt before you decide whether it's safe to carry on driving!

Broken coolant pump drivebelt	Don't drive the car. If you do, the engine will overheat very quickly.
Broken alternator drivebelt	It's OK to drive on for a short distance. The alternator won't charge the battery, so the alternator warning light will come on and the battery will soon go flat, at which stage the engine will stop.
Broken power steering pump drivebelt	It's OK to drive the car. You'll still be able to steer, but you may need a lot of effort to turn the steering wheel.
Broken air conditioning compressor drivebelt	It's OK to drive the car, but the air conditioning won't work.
Broken fuel injection pump drivebelt (diesel engines)	The engine will stop, so you won't be able to drive the car! Fitting a new injection pump drivebelt isn't a job which can be done at the roadside, so you'll need to call for help.
Broken vacuum pump drivebelt (diesel engines)	It's OK to drive the car. The brakes will still work, but you'll need to push the brake pedal harder than normal to stop the car.
Broken hydraulic pump drivebelt (some middle-sized and all larger Citroëns)	Don't drive the car. The brakes will stop working after a few applications and the suspension will be down on its stops.

BATTERIES

Always check your battery before the start of winter. During winter the battery is under extra strain when it has to start the car on cold, damp mornings. You're also likely to be using more electrical equipment in winter – heater, heated rear window, wipers, lights, etc.

Is the battery flat?

If the lights have been left on, you may find that there isn't enough power to turn the starter motor. You may even find that the warning lights don't come on when you turn the key.

The first sign of a failing battery is a sluggish starter motor. Turn on the headlights, and then operate the starter. If the headlights dim, or go out, it's probably a battery problem; it's worth getting the system checked by an auto-electrician.

If you have a test meter, you can test the battery output, but this will only be accurate if the battery has not been used for 6 hours. Connect the meter across the terminals (connecting the red lead to the positive terminal). If the battery is in good condition, the reading should be above 12.5 volts. If the reading is 12.2 to 12.4 volts, the battery is partially discharged, and if the reading is less than 12.2 volts, the battery is flat.

1. Call for assistance. If you're a member of one of the motoring breakdown organisations, they may even come to your house – check your membership documents for details.
2. Use jump leads to start the car – see "How to use jump leads".
3. Charge the battery. You won't be able to start the car until the battery is charged, so if you want to use it straight away, you'll need to use one of the previous methods, then charge the battery later. If you drive the car a reasonable distance (say 20 miles or more), the alternator will charge the battery for you; fewer miles will mean the same starting problems next time.

SIMPLE CHECKS AND SERVICING

How to check a battery

Make sure that the battery tray is in good condition, and that the securing clamp is tight. Corrosion can be removed with a solution of water and baking soda. Rinse with water. Any metal damaged by corrosion should be covered with a zinc-based primer, then painted.

1 Check the outside of the battery for damage. Check the tightness of the cable clamps to ensure good connections. You shouldn't be able to move them. Also check each cable for cracks and fraying.

2 If the cable clamps are corroded (white fluffy deposits), disconnect the cables, clean them with a wire brush, then refit them. You can keep corrosion on the terminals to a minimum by applying petroleum jelly, or terminal protector, after reconnecting them.

3 Check the battery negative lead connection to the body or the engine, as applicable. If necessary, unbolt the lead and clean the connector and the area on the body or engine, then bolt the lead into position.

4 If your battery is maintenance-free, there may be a condition indicator fitted to indicate its charge condition. Check your car's handbook, or the battery instructions, for details of how to use the indicator.

5 If your battery isn't maintenance-free, check the electrolyte every few months; this will tell you the battery condition. To do this, you'll need to use a hydrometer – follow the manufacturer's instructions.

AIR FILTER RENEWAL

The filter stops dirt and dust from being sucked into the engine. If the element's very dirty or blocked, the engine won't run properly, and the fuel consumption might be higher than normal. If the filter is missing or split, dirt may be sucked into the engine, causing expensive damage. When buying a new air filter, you'll need to know the model, engine size and year of manufacture of your car.
Renew the air filter at the manufacturer's recommended intervals, typically every 24,000 miles or two years.

Air filters are usually housed in a rectangular casing next to the engine, or a round casing on top of the engine.

FUEL FILTER RENEWAL – PETROL ENGINES

Some older cars don't have a fuel filter, but all modern cars, and all cars with fuel injection, do. The fuel filter stops any dirt in the fuel from getting into the fuel system. The dirt could otherwise cause blockages, which would make the engine run badly, or not at all, and possibly cause expensive damage. After a period of time, the filter will become full of dirt, and the fuel won't pass through it properly. To prevent problems, the filter must be renewed at the recommended intervals. The fuel filter should be renewed at the manufacturer's recommended intervals (usually around every 60,000 miles).

FUEL FILTER DRAINING AND RENEWAL – DIESEL ENGINES

The fuel filter stops any dirt in the fuel from getting into the fuel injection system. The dirt could otherwise cause blockages, which would make the engine run badly, or not at all, and possibly cause expensive damage. After a period of time, the filter will become full of dirt, and the fuel won't pass through it properly.

As well as filtering out dirt, most fuel filter assemblies incorporate a water separator to prevent any water in the fuel from getting into the fuel system components.

The fuel filter should be renewed at the manufacturer's recommended intervals (typically around every 18,000 miles).

Water should be drained from the fuel filter assembly at least every 6000 miles or 6 months, or as soon as the "water in fuel" warning light (if fitted) comes on. It should also be drained at the beginning of winter in order to avoid problems caused by the water freezing.

TIMING BELT RENEWAL

A timing belt drives the engine camshaft(s) from the crankshaft. The timing belt runs around sprockets on the crankshaft and camshaft(s), and may also drive engine ancillaries.

A tensioner is fitted to keep the belt tight. The tensioner may be automatic, or it could be manually-adjustable.

Timing belts don't last for the lifetime of the car, and must be renewed at or before the recommended intervals – if a timing belt breaks when the engine is running, it could cause very serious engine damage.

Not all cars have timing belts – some may have a timing chain instead. Often, the engine specifications in your car's handbook will tell you whether the engine has "belt-driven" or "chain-driven" camshaft(s) – if not, contact an authorised dealer or your car manufacturer to find out.

The pollen filter should be renewed at the manufacturer's recommended intervals (usually around 20,000 miles or 2 years).

POLLEN FILTER RENEWAL

Some cars are fitted with a pollen filter to filter the air which goes into the heating/ventilation system. The filter will stop pollen and dust from the atmosphere being drawn into the car's interior.

MANUAL TRANSMISSION OIL LEVEL CHECK

If the oil level gets low, the transmission may become noisy, and you might have trouble selecting gears. (Note though that gear selection trouble can also be caused by clutch problems.) If the level gets too low, the transmission may be damaged.

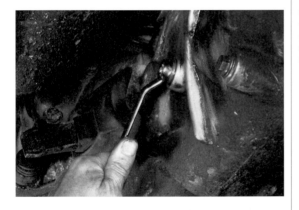

On most transmissions, the oil level is checked using a level hole in the side of the transmission casing.

The oil level should be checked at the manufacturer's recommended intervals (usually around every 12,000 miles or 12 months), but note that some cars have "sealed-for-life" transmissions, and there's no way of checking the oil level. You should also have the oil level checked if you suspect that there's a leak.

On some cars the transmission oil should be renewed at the manufacturer's recommended intervals – often around every 60,000 miles.

AUTOMATIC TRANSMISSION FLUID LEVEL CHECK

If the automatic transmission fluid level gets low, the transmission may not work properly – low fluid level is a common source of problems with automatic transmissions. If the level gets too low, it could damage the transmission.

If frequent topping-up is needed, have the cause found and fixed without delay.

The automatic transmission fluid should be checked at the manufacturer's recommended intervals (at least every 6,000 miles or 12 months).

Check the automatic transmission fluid level with a level dipstick which fits inside a tube attached to the transmission. The level is usually checked with the transmission warm, after a short drive. Have the transmission oil renewed at the manufacturer's recommended intervals (usually around every 30,000 miles).

REAR FINAL DRIVE OIL LEVEL CHECK

On rear-wheel-drive cars, if the final drive oil level gets low, the final drive (differential) may become noisy. If the level gets very low, the differential may be damaged. (On front-wheel-drive cars, the final drive is integral with the transmission.)

On most final drives, the oil level is checked using a level hole in the final drive casing.

The final drive oil level should be checked at the manufacturer's recommended intervals (typically around every 12,000 miles or 12 months, although some manufacturers don't specify a level check). You should also check the level if the back axle becomes noisy (whining or rumbling noises), or if there's evidence of oil leakage (oily areas on the back axle or oil droppings under the back of the car). On some cars, the final drive oil should be renewed at the manufacturer's recommended intervals – often around 60,000 miles.

ROAD TEST

Carrying out a road test will help you to spot any problems which show up only when the car is being driven. Be careful not to inconvenience other traffic when carrying out the test.

1 With the engine stopped, press the brake pedal four or five times to exhaust the vacuum in the servo, then hold it down. Start the engine, and the pedal should 'give' slightly. Run the engine for a couple of minutes, then switch off. Pump the brake pedal four or five times again – you should hear a slight hiss each time the pedal is pressed down. After pressing four or five times, there should be no further hissing, and the pedal should feel firm when you press it again. If the brake pedal does not operate as described, you may have a faulty brake vacuum servo, which you should have checked as soon as possible.

2 Check that the handbrake works properly, without the lever having to be pulled up too far. Check that the handbrake holds the car safely on a slope.

3 Now start the test drive. Make sure that the car doesn't pull to one side when braking, and check that there's no vibration through the steering or brake pedal when braking.

4 Check for any strange 'feel', vibration or noises in the steering and suspension, especially when driving over bumps and round corners.

5 Make sure that the engine starts easily when hot and cold, and that it runs smoothly when idling.

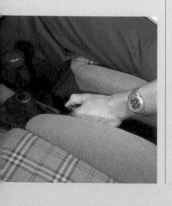

6 Listen for any strange noises from the engine and transmission.

7 Check that the clutch pedal moves smoothly, and that the clutch is not jerky and does not slip (if the clutch slips, then engine revs will rise unexpectedly when pulling away or when changing gear).

8 Check that all the gears can be engaged smoothly without noise, and that the gear lever is smooth and not 'notchy' or 'vague' when you move it.

9 Listen for a clicking or knocking noise when driving slowly with the steering on full lock. Any noise indicates wear in the driveshaft joints.

10 Check that the instruments and warning lights on the dashboard all work, and check that all the electrical equipment (lights, wipers, etc) works with the engine running.

11 If you find any problems, have them checked and fixed as soon as possible.

THE BODYWORK AND THE INTERIOR

Cleaning your car's bodywork and interior regularly is a good way of preserving its value. Some people swear that their car actually runs better when it's just been washed – that's unlikely to be literally true, but it stands to reason that you'll feel better about driving a sparkling clean vehicle than you will if it's plastered with what is politely known as "road dirt". Your passengers probably prefer to be in clean surroundings too, though anyone who regularly transports small (and not so small) children will know that keeping the car free of sticky debris is a full-time job.

In this chapter we give you some tips on various cleaning and restoration techniques, including how to touch up the inevitable paint chips and minor scars.

HOW TO WASH YOUR CAR

This is the most important thing you can do to protect the paintwork. You'll also spot any stone chips or damage before rust starts to take hold. Don't use household detergents – they're much too harsh, and they can damage the paint. Don't wash the car in bright sunlight, because the water will dry almost straight away, giving a blotchy finish. Cold water on hot paint can cause tiny cracks in the finish.

1 Rinse the car first using cold water with a bucket and sponge to get rid of dirt and mud, and scrub the wheels. Thick mud can be soaked off using a hose. Rinse out the bucket, then pour in the recommended amount of soap and fill the bucket with cold water. Don't use too much soap, it will be hard to rinse off and will leave a smeary film.

2 Use a proper car soap or shampoo, which will usually contain wax. This will thoroughly clean the paintwork, and you'll end up with a nice shiny finish.

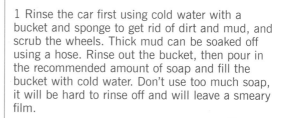

3 Soap the car using a soft, clean sponge, then rinse with cold water. Dry off using a chamois leather, which will absorb the water, and give a shiny finish without streaks.

HOW TO POLISH YOUR CAR

If you find that the water no longer "beads" on your car's paintwork when it rains, or when you wash it, a coat of polish wouldn't hurt!

Most modern polishes use wax and/or silicone, and these clean the paintwork, and leave a layer of protective wax on top. Read the label to make sure that the polish is suitable for your car – for example, some polishes can't be used on metallic paintwork. Many paint finishes use two coats, a base colour coat, with a clear coat of resin over the top - don't use abrasive polishes on these finishes, or you'll remove the clear coat. Don't polish in strong sunlight. If you do, the polish will dry immediately, and it will be hard to remove (you may even end up scratching the paint trying to get the polish off). Before you start, wash the car, and thoroughly dry it. You'll need two soft cloths: one for applying the polish, and one for buffing-off. Cotton cloths are best to avoid the problem of bits of cloth sticking to the paint as you polish.

It's best to work on one panel at a time – if you try to put polish on the whole car, then buff it off, the polish you put on first will have dried by the time you come to buff it off. Apply a light even layer of polish, using a light circular motion, then let it dry to a haze (not a white powder), and lightly buff it off using your buffing cloth. If you get polish on the glass, rub it off straight away unless the label says it's suitable for glass – most polishes aren't.

If the polish gets onto plastic trim panels, it can discolour them when it dries. You can get rid of these marks using a grease or wax remover (available from most car accessory shops), but read the label to make sure that it's suitable, and follow the instructions.

You can restore the look of plastic trim parts using a plastic cleaner or colour restorer (again, read the instructions). These can work wonders with faded plastic, but make sure you wipe any overspill off the paintwork straight away.

TOUCH-UP PAINT

Every car has a paint code, which is usually stamped onto a metal plate when the car is painted at the factory. If you're going to buy paint from an official parts dealer, take your car along – the staff will know where to find the code, often on a plate under the bonnet.

Car accessory shops also sell touch-up paint; all you need to know is the manufacturer's name for the paint colour, and when the car was built. Although these paints are usually a close match to the original, they're rarely exact matches. If you want to be sure of an exact colour match, you should always buy the paint from a dealer for your make of car.

You can usually buy touch-up paint in two forms: the easy-to-use "touch-up stick", or a spray-can. The stick consists of a small canister of paint, with a brush built into the lid. Sometimes you'll also get a wire brush for removing rust and flaky paint from the scratch, but take care if you decide to use it – the sharp bristles can make a mess of perfectly good paint.

Rust

If you've got major rust problems, you'll need the help of a bodywork expert, but small rust spots are quite easy to fix.

If you notice a rust spot when you're cleaning the car, it's best to get rid of it as soon as you can, before it develops into a more serious problem.

There are many rust treatment kits available from car accessory shops; follow the instructions.

How to touch-up paint chips and scratches

Use the wire brush supplied with the touch-up stick, or a small piece of fine wire wool, to remove any rust. Try not to damage the good paintwork around the scratch (wrapping wire wool around the end of a pencil helps).

Next, clean around the scratch. It's best to use plain water, anything else might damage the paintwork, or stop the new paint sticking. Let the paintwork dry fully.

The paint must be thoroughly mixed, usually by shaking the touch-up stick for a few minutes; follow the instructions. Apply a small amount of paint, using the touch-up stick brush or, better still, a very fine artist's brush. Work slowly, and brush one way. Try to "fill" the scratch – don't let the new paint build up higher than the good paint around the scratch. With a two-coat finish, follow the instructions and apply the clear coat after the colour coat has dried properly.

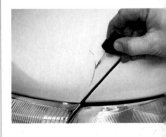

Wait a few days for the paint to dry properly, then rub the painted area using a polishing compound (or a very mild abrasive colour restorer) to blend in the new paint. Once you're happy with the result, wash and polish the car to finish off.

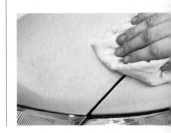

Matt paint?

As your car gets older, the paintwork might start to fade, looking dull and dirty even after you've washed it.

As long as things haven't got too bad, you should be able to revive the paint using a colour restorer. You can buy a whole range of restorers: some are more abrasive than others, some are especially for metallic paint, and some are coloured for use on a certain paint colour. All these products work by removing a layer of paint, so take care!

It's best to start off with a restorer which is only mildly abrasive. Paint is easy to take off, but you can't put it back on! Try it out on a small area first to see what the results will be before you start on a large panel – don't rub too hard, some remove paint very quickly.

You'll need plenty of soft cloths. Use separate cloths for applying the colour restorer, and for buffing-off. Changing the cloths as they become covered with paint. Cotton cloths are best to avoid the problem of bits of cloth sticking to the paint as you work.

Once you're satisfied with the results, apply a coat of polish.

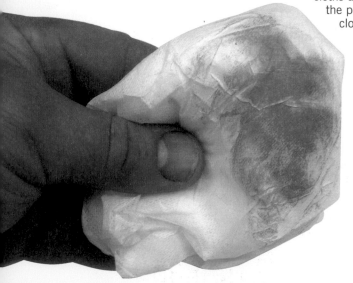

WHEELS

Spoked wheels aren't seen very much these days, which is just as well - they looked pretty, but they were expensive to produce and difficult to maintain, as anyone who has tried to true-up a bicycle wheel will testify.

The wheels on modern cars are made of pressed steel or aluminium; they are strong, light and sometimes decorative, but they still need a certain amount of looking after, mostly for cosmetic reasons.

WARNING
When you're cleaning wheels, take care not to breathe in brake dust, as it can be dangerous to health.

Cleaning alloy wheels

Using an alloy wheel cleaner solution and a soft-bristled brush should get rid of most of the dirt. Always follow the instructions on the packaging when using wheel cleaner – some cleaners are caustic, in which case wear gloves, and don't get the cleaner on the car's paintwork. Once you've got alloy wheels clean, polishing them will make dirt easier to remove in the future. You can use a special alloy wheel polish, or if your wheels have a clear-coat finish applied over the metal, ordinary wax car polish will give good results.

Touching-up alloy wheels

Most alloy wheels have a clear-coat finish applied to the metal. If the clear-coat finish gets chipped, it's a good idea to repair the chipped area before the exposed alloy becomes stained or oxidised.

1 Clean the wheel using alloy wheel cleaner, then rinse the wheel and thoroughly dry it.

2 Clean and polish the exposed alloy using fine (400-grade) emery paper, or a fine scouring pad. Carefully feather the edges of the clear-coat surrounding the affected area, then wipe clean with a dry cloth.

3 Use a fine artist's brush to apply the clear-coat (follow the preparation instructions on the packaging). Apply several thin coats to blend in with the surrounding area.

How to avoid losing wheel covers

Unclip the wheel cover, and check for any broken clips. If a clip is badly broken, or if several clips are broken, you may have no option but to renew the cover.

Buy a few long cable-ties, of a colour suitable for your wheel covers. If the wheel covers have holes in them, feed a cable-tie through one of the holes in the cover. Loop the cable-tie round behind the wheel, and push it back out through another suitable hole in the wheel cover.

Fasten the ends of the cable-tie together, then pull tight, and cut off the excess.

You can hide the joined ends of the cable-tie by sliding the cable-tie round so that the ends are behind the wheel cover.

If your wheel trims don't have any holes, you can still secure them using cable-ties, but secure the cable-ties to the clips on the back of the wheel covers.

Remember that the wheel cover will have to be removed to change the wheel, so carry a suitable tool to cut the cable tie.

Cleaning steel wheels and covers

Cleaning with car shampoo and a sponge should give acceptable results. Any stubborn dirt can be removed using a brush, and if necessary a wheel cleaner spray (check that it's suitable for use on plastic components, if applicable – most alloy wheel cleaners aren't).

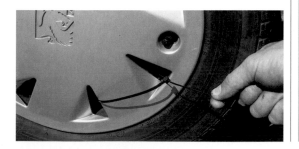

FIXING LOOSE TRIM

If you find that a piece of trim is loose, it's worth taking the time to fix it before it falls off. Most trim parts are held on with clips or strong adhesive tape. Never try to glue it back into position – the repair probably won't last long, and you may damage the paintwork.

Trim panels secured by adhesive tape

You can buy special trim tape from car accessory shops. In many cases, it's best to pull the trim right off, and reattach it using new tape. Once you've removed the trim, you need to clean off all the old adhesive; it can be difficult, so you might need to buy adhesive remover (follow the instructions supplied).

1 To line up the trim when you refit it, you can stick masking tape along the body. Align it with other trim strips, or measure from the edge of the panel to make sure it's straight.

2 Cut the adhesive tape as necessary, and stick it to the back of the trim or the bodywork. On wide trim strips, you'll have to use two strips of tape side-by-side. Hold the trim in position, and check that the tape is thick enough to stick the trim to the body. Sometimes you'll need a double thickness of tape.

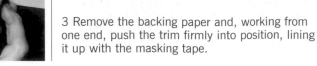

3 Remove the backing paper and, working from one end, push the trim firmly into position, lining it up with the masking tape.

THE BODYWORK AND THE **INTERIOR**

Trim panels secured by clips

If you find that a clip's broken,
you might have to release the
surrounding clips to
pull the trim away to
fit the new clip.
Take care, it's very
easy to break more
clips.
You should be
able to buy new
clips from your local
parts dealer.
Make sure that
you get the
correct clip.
Fit the new clip,
then fit the panel
back into
position.

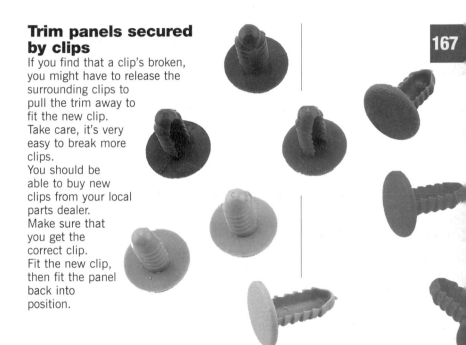

Squeaky doors

A squeaky door is almost bound to be dry
hinges. This is fixed by opening the door, and
oiling or greasing the hinges, using a multi-
purpose grease. An aerosol lubricant will
usually work wonders too. Once you've
applied the grease or spray, open and close
the door a few times to work the lubricant into
the hinges. Wipe off any excess grease or
spray to stop it finding its way onto the
bodywork and trim, and your clothes.

INTERIOR

A regular clearout and clean-up is easier than an annual blitz and will keep your car looking good. Try to pick a fine day as you'll need to have the doors open. You will need a vacuum cleaner, duster/polishing cloths and spray-on cleaner (various types of spray-on cleaner are available from car accessory shops - choose whatever suits your needs).

First of all, take out all the loose items you've been carrying around. Remove the floor mats, if fitted, empty the ashtrays, and pull out the stereo unit if it's the removable kind.

Open all the doors wide, and vacuum up any loose dirt, grit, etc. Don't forget to vacuum in between and underneath the front seats. Try to use a separate brush attachment for the seats. While you're using the vacuum cleaner, carry on and clean the boot. If your car has folding rear seats, lift the cushion(s) and clean underneath.

Inspect the carpets, if you find any stains, use a spray-on cleaner, working it in with a nail-brush and vacuuming or sponging off, according to the instructions. You'll probably find the worst ground-in dirt on the driver's side carpet, especially near the pedals.

Check seats for marks and use fabric cleaner to deal with these. Allow any dampened seats and carpets to dry before using the car. If you have access to a suitable wet-and-dry vacuum cleaner, this can be used to speed up the drying.

Now that the dust-raising is over, you can finish off with the interior trim. Use a soft duster to remove the surface dust before cleaning with a suitable trim cleaner. As well as removing grime, these normally help to keep the car smelling fresh. Windows are best cleaned using a chamois leather, but difficult marks can be removed with a glass cleaner, buffing finally with a soft cloth.

THE BODYWORK AND THE **INTERIOR**

Getting rid of smells

If the problem is due to spillage, you'll need to clean the affected area using a suitable cleaner – see "Interior".

Depending on the type of spillage, you may need to clean the affected area with disinfectant first, but read the instructions on the label to make sure that it won't damage the relevant trim.

Once you've got rid of the source of trouble, you may still be left with an unpleasant smell. Parking the car with the windows open should help to reduce the problem.

Most car accessory shops sell a range of air fresheners for cars. You should be able to buy one with "odour-neutralising" properties which will help to get rid of any lingering smells. Read the the packaging to decide which product is the best for your needs.

Cleaning plastic trim parts

Use a suitable plastic cleaner, which you can buy from car accessory shops. Read the instructions on the label when you're choosing a cleaner, because not all cleaners are suitable for all plastics.

When using cleaners or restorers on the plastic trim panels, it's best to apply the cleaner or restorer to a clean cloth, then use the cloth to rub it onto the plastic, this will help to avoid getting plastic cleaner or restorer on the paintwork. Wipe any overspill off the paintwork straight away.

PREPARING
FOR THE MOT
TEST

All cars over 3 years old must have an MoT test annually. It's an offence to use such a car on the road without a current test certificate (except when driving to or from a test). The test certificate will also have to be produced when buying the Road Fund Licence ('car tax'). Although it may seem an annoying formality, the test is an important contribution to road safety.

Not everybody realises that they are entitled to watch the test being carried out. If you're interested enough to do this, you may pick up some useful information about the general mechanical condition of your car. A friendly tester will sometimes point out items which, although not part of the test, could require attention soon.

Obviously it won't be possible for you to examine the car to the same standard as the professional MoT tester. However, working through the following checks will help you to identify some of the possible problem areas before taking the car for the test.

Basics
If you do nothing else, at least clean the car thoroughly inside and out, and preferably give the underside a wash too. The tester can refuse to examine a car which is really filthy underneath. If the car is clean and looks well cared-for, the tester may be more likely to pass a borderline component than if the car is scruffy and apparently neglected.

The following pages give a summary of the test requirements, based on the regulations at the time of printing.

It won't be possible for you to carry out all the checks which will be done by the MoT tester, as some of them are quite involved, and require special equipment. You will be able to spot most of the more common problems which might cause a car to fail, by carrying out the following checks. Other checks, which require the car to be raised, are beyond the scope of this book.

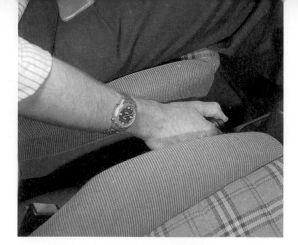

CHECKS CARRIED OUT FROM THE DRIVER'S SEAT

Handbrake

Check that the handbrake works correctly. If you have to pull the lever a long way up (too many clicks), the cable probably needs adjustment. Check that the handbrake can't be released by tapping the lever sideways. Check that the lever mountings are secure.

Footbrake

Check that the brake pedal is secure and in good condition. Check for signs of brake fluid leaks on the pedal, floor or carpets. Press the brake pedal and check that it doesn't move down as far as the floor. Release the pedal, wait a few seconds, then push it again. If the pedal travels nearly to the floor before firm resistance is felt, brake adjustment or repair is necessary. If the pedal feels spongy, there is air in the hydraulic system which must be removed by bleeding. Check the brake servo unit by pushing the brake pedal several times, then keeping the pedal pushed down and starting the engine. As the engine starts, the pedal will move down slightly. If not, the servo may be faulty.

Steering wheel and column

Check the steering wheel for damage. Check that the steering wheel is not loose on the column, and that there is no abnormal movement of the steering wheel, indicating wear in the column support bearings or joints.

Windscreen and mirrors

There must be no cracks or large chips in the glass within the driver's field of view. (Small stone chips are acceptable.) Rear view mirrors must be securely fixed, the glass must be in good condition, and it must be possible to adjust the mirrors.

Doors

Both front doors must be able to be opened and closed from outside and inside, and must latch securely when closed.

Electrical equipment

Switch on the ignition and check that the horn works. Check the windscreen washers and wipers, and check the wiper blades (see "Windscreen wiper check and renewal"); renew damaged or perished blades.
Also check the operation of the brake lights.

Seat belts and seats

Check the seat belts (see "Seat belts"). The front seats themselves must be securely attached and the backrests must lock in the upright position.

CHECKS CARRIED OUT WITH THE CAR ON THE GROUND

Vehicle identification

Number plates must be in good condition, securely fitted and easily readable, with letters and numbers correctly spaced.

The vehicle identification number on the plate under the bonnet must be readable.

Electrical equipment

Check the operation of all the lights (see "Bulb check"). Also check that the lenses and reflectors are clean and undamaged.

Braking system

Check all the brake components, brake pipes and servo unit for leaks, loose mountings, corrosion or other damage. The fluid reservoir must be secure and the fluid level correct (see "Brake fluid level check"). Check both front brake hoses for cracks or deterioration of the rubber. Turn the steering from lock-to-lock, and make sure that the hoses don't touch the wheel, tyre, or any part of the steering or suspension mechanism. With the brake pedal firmly pressed, check the hoses for bulges or leaks.

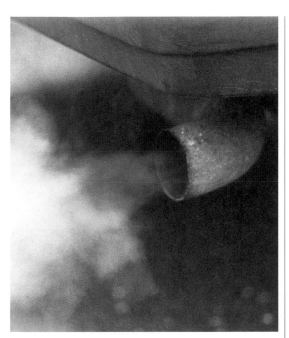

Exhaust system

Start the engine. With your assistant holding a cloth over the tailpipe, check the entire system for leaks. You will be able to hear if the system is leaking. If there are no leaks, the engine will stall if the cloth is held over the end of the exhaust for more than a few seconds.

Steering and suspension

Carry out the checks which can be done without jacking up the car (see "How to check the shock absorbers"). If power steering is fitted, check that the pump is secure and free from leaks, and check the condition of the auxiliary drivebelt (see "Checking an auxiliary drivebelt"). Check that the car is standing level when parked.

WHERE DO I GO FOR HELP?

This chapter gives some hints on choosing a garage and on communicating your requirements. If you can explain clearly what your problem is or what work you expect to have done, there's less chance of an unpleasant surprise when you receive the bill. There's also some information on warranties and pointers to the best places to buy consumables such as tyres and exhaust systems.

CHOOSING A GARAGE

If you need to have work done on your car, whether it's servicing, repair work, or fitting extras, how do you decide where to take it? You may decide to carry out the work yourself, or you may have a suitably-qualified friend who's willing to help; otherwise you'll need to find a garage to do the work for you.

If your car is still under warranty, always take it to an authorised dealer for any work or checks to be carried out; if you take it anywhere else, you may invalidate the warranty.

If you want to ensure that your car has an authentic service history when you come to sell it, then you may decide to have all work done by an authorised dealer. Generally, this will be the most expensive option, but you'll have the satisfaction of knowing that genuine manufacturer's procedures and parts will be used for all the work.

If your car needs tyres, exhaust parts, shock absorbers, or even a new clutch, it's worth trying one of the specialist fitting centres. Many will offer you an all-inclusive price for a particular job, often with a comprehensive warranty, and for far less than a garage.

If you're not prepared to pay the rates charged by an authorised dealer, you may decide to take your car to one of the smaller independent garages. Some specialise in a particular make of car and, although they may not be authorised dealers, you'll often find that their expertise is equal to that of the manufacturer's trained personnel. If you're going to take your car to an independent garage, it's always worth visiting several in your area, and asking them for a price for the work to be carried out. Always ask for a written firm price, and check to see what's included (see "How much will it cost?").

Does the garage have a good reputation?

Pay a visit to the garage, and talk to one of the mechanics to get a feel for the enthusiasm and knowledge of the staff, and the standard of service. There's no reason to treat small garages with suspicion, many provide a better service than authorised dealers, but unfortunately there are still a few rogues around who will take advantage of the unwary. At a smaller garage, you can't always expect the "fancy" service provided by a larger dealer; there may not be a carpeted waiting area, and you may not be provided with a courtesy car, but remember that a dealer is building these "perks" into your bill.

Ask around to see if anyone you know has had good or bad experience of dealing with any of the garages you're thinking of using. Reputation is very important, and it's often better to pay a little extra to take your car to a garage with a known good reputation.

Understanding the mechanic

When you're talking about any work to be done on your car, don't let yourself be baffled. "Glossary" should help you to understand the terminology used, and the explanations of how systems work should be useful too. Make sure that you understand what work the garage is intending to do. Ask if there may be any problems; for instance, there can be seized or broken fasteners to contend with, which may make the job more difficult.

Sometimes, a mechanic may point out other potential problems whilst carrying out work on your car. The mechanic might suggest that you'll need a set of brake discs and pads soon. Always check this for yourself, or ask the mechanic to show you the problem. If in doubt, ask for a second opinion from an experienced friend or another garage.

EXPLAINING A PROBLEM

If you've got a problem with your car, how do you explain it to the service manager or mechanic at the local garage? Remember that most garages will charge you at an hourly rate, so any extra information is likely to save you money in the long run.

If you haven't been able to identify a problem, here are a few things which you're likely to be asked when you take your car to the garage.

- Does the problem occur all the time, or is it intermittent?
- Does the problem occur when the engine's cold, hot or both?
- Are there any other symptoms (noises, vibration, etc)?
- Has the car been regularly serviced?
- Have you had any work carried out on the car recently?

If the problem occurs all the time, the best thing is to take the mechanic out for a drive and demonstrate it.

Intermittent problems can be difficult to trace and cure. If the problem is present for a while before disappearing, take the car to the garage when the problem is present. Most mechanical problems will be relatively easy to trace, but engine problems can be tricky. Sometimes the garage may have no option but to renew various components until the problem disappears – this could prove to be expensive.

Always ask for a written firm price (sometimes it may not be possible to give an accurate final price), otherwise you may be faced with a large unexpected bill.

HOW MUCH WILL IT COST?

Whenever you're intending to get any work done, get a written firm price before you agree. It's always wise to get rough prices from several different garages so that you can compare them. Beware of verbal prices, particularly over the telephone; if your bill turns out to be more than expected, you won't have a case to argue unless you have a written firm price.

What's included?

The items on a garage bill usually fall into one of three categories: parts, labour and consumables. Parts include any new parts which may be required during the work. Labour covers the cost of the time taken (in hours) by the mechanic to carry out the work. Consumables cover items such oil, coolant, cleaning fluids, etc.

Always ask for an itemised list so that you can see exactly what's been included.

Here are a few things which you should ask when getting a price for a job:

- What's the hourly labour rate?
- How long should the work take?
- Will genuine or pattern parts be used?
- Is VAT included?
- Will the work be covered by a warranty? (Ask for details of the warranty)

Comparing rough prices for work

Be sure that you're making a fair comparison, as the prices may be structured differently.

You can check the cost of genuine parts by asking at an authorised dealer, or of pattern parts from a motor factor. A garage will almost certainly pay a "trade" price for parts which will always be less than the "retail" price.

If you're having any new parts fitted, check whether the work will be covered by a parts and labour warranty; if not, ask why.

You should find that the prices are similar and, by comparing them, you'll be able to spot any discrepancies or suspicious costs. Ask if there's anything you don't understand.

Once you decide to have the work done, ask the garage to contact you immediately if they encounter any problems which will involve additional work.

If you don't do this, many will carry out the work anyway, and charge you accordingly.

CHECKING THE BILL

Always ask for an itemised bill, which will give you a full breakdown of all the costs, and will allow you to see exactly what work has been carried out.

* Check the details of the bill against the firm price, and query any discrepancies. If you find that "miscellaneous" costs appear on your bill, ask what they are.
* Check the labour costs against the garage's quoted hourly rate, and check the price of any parts used (see "What's included?").
* Check that the work described on the bill has been carried out (see "Checking the work"), and if there's any evidence that you've been billed for work which hasn't been done, query it with the mechanic concerned.

Once you've checked the bill, and you're happy that it's accurate, it's time to dip into your bank account!

CHECKING THE WORK

If components have been renewed, many garages leave the old components in a box in the boot so that you can see that the work has been carried out, and was necessary. It's a good idea to ask the mechanic to do this when you take your car in for work to be done.

If your car has been serviced, check that a new (clean) oil filter has been fitted, and pull out the dipstick to check for fresh oil. You should be able to tell where work has been done, because the area around the work should be cleaner than the rest of the car.

If the work involved disturbing any gaskets or seals, park the car overnight with a sheet of card or paper underneath (or pick a clean piece of road or driveway) so that you can check for signs of leaks in the morning. If you notice any leaks, take the car back to have them fixed, and don't let the garage charge you for fixing the problem (unless it's totally unrelated to the work they've done).

If the work involved removing the wheels, it's a good idea to check that you can remove the wheel nuts or bolts to change a wheel (see "How to change a wheel").

WARRANTIES

Whenever you buy a new or second-hand car, a warranty should be included. Similarly, when you have any work carried out, the work should be covered by a warranty.

The warranties provided with new cars are normally very comprehensive, and often include membership of one of the breakdown organisations. You may be offered the chance to take out an "extended warranty" on a new car. Always check carefully what's covered by an extended warranty (is there a claim limit, and is anything excluded?), and weigh this up against the cost. An extended warranty can be a very expensive way of buying peace-of-mind, especially if it ties you to having the car serviced by the dealer.

When buying a second-hand car, always check what sort of warranty you're getting. You'll generally find that there's a maximum claim limit, which is often so low that it effectively limits claims to very minor problems. If you have to pay extra for a warranty, read the small-print very carefully – you'll probably find that it's not worth the extra cost.

If you have any work done which involves the fitting of new components (especially major items such as an engine or gearbox), make sure that the work is covered by a parts and labour warranty. This will cover you against the use of any faulty parts, and any mistakes made by the mechanic which might cause trouble later. Check that the bill states the work is covered by a warranty, and be sure the warranty period is specified.

BUYING PARTS

To be sure of obtaining the correct parts, you'll need to know the model and year of manufacture of your car, and it will sometimes be necessary to quote the Vehicle Identification Number (VIN). Your car's handbook will usually show you where to find the VIN. It can also be useful to take the old parts along for identification. Parts such as starter motors and alternators may be available under a service exchange.

Accessory shops
These are good for components needed for car maintenance. Items of this sort from a reputable shop are usually of the same standard as those used by the car manufacturer.
Besides components, these shops also sell tools and general accessories, have convenient opening hours and charge lower prices. Some accessory shops have parts counters where components needed for almost any repair job can be bought or ordered.

Motor factors

Good factors will stock all the more important components which wear out comparatively quickly, and can supply individual parts needed for the overhaul of a larger assembly (eg, brake seals and hydraulic parts, engine bearing shells, pistons, valves, etc).

Tyre and exhaust specialists

These may be independent, or members of a chain. They frequently offer competitive prices when compared with a dealer or local garage. When researching prices, also ask what "extras" may be added - fitting a valve and wheel balancing are often both charged on top of the price of a new tyre.

Other sources

Beware of parts or materials bought from market stalls, car boot sales, etc. These items aren't necessarily sub-standard, but there's little chance of compensation if they are unsatisfactory. In the case of safety-critical components such as brake pads, there's also the risk of a failure causing injury or death. Second-hand components obtained from a car breaker can be a good buy in some circumstances, but this sort of purchase is best made by an experienced DIY mechanic.

WHERE DO I GO FOR HELP?

Officially appointed garages

This is the best source for parts which are peculiar to your car (eg, badges, interior trim, body panels, etc). It's the only place you should buy parts if your car is still under warranty.

BUYING AND SELLING A **CAR**

Before buying a second-hand car, it's worth doing some homework to try and avoid some of the pitfalls that await the unwary. First of all, don't rush out and buy the first car that catches your eye (all that glitters is not gold!), and remember that much of the responsibility is yours when it comes to the soundness of the deal, especially when buying a car privately.

Advertising

Once you've decided on the asking price, you need to advertise. Local newspapers and magazines are probably your best bet, although if you want to reach a more specific audience, place an advert in one of the specialist car sales papers or magazines. Think carefully about the wording of your advert. You need to give as much positive information as possible, without using too many words (especially if you are paying on a per word basis!) Give details of the model and engine size, service history (where applicable), colour, age, mileage, condition and any desirable options or equipment. If you've owned the car from new, make sure you add the words, "one owner".

If you're trading the car in with a dealer, you will probably get a lower price than if you sell privately. If selling privately, don't allow the buyer to take the car away until you have their money, and it's a good idea to ask them to sign a piece of paper to say that they're happy to buy the car as viewed, just in case any problems develop later on. Give a receipt for the money paid.

SELLING A CAR

If you're going to sell your car, the first thing to do is to decide what price to ask. There are car price guides available from newsagents. The price you can expect depends on the car's age, condition and mileage. Don't ask too much, but it may be a good idea to ask for more than you're prepared to accept, then there's some room for negotiation between you and the buyer.

Once you're decided on how much to ask for your car, you need to advertise it. Local papers and magazines carry advertisements for a reasonable cost. If you want to reach a more specific audience, place an advert in one of the specialist car sales papers or magazines.

Think about the wording of your advert. You need to give as much positive information as possible, without using too many words. Give details of the model and engine size, service history (where applicable), colour, age, mileage, condition and any desirable options or equipment. If you've owned the car from new, it's always worth stating "one owner".

Bear in mind the points which the prospective buyer should be looking for, as described in "Buying second-hand". It goes without saying that the car should be clean and tidy, as first impressions are important. Any fluid leaks should be cured, and there's no point in trying to disguise any major bodywork or mechanical problems.

Make sure that the service documents, registration document, etc, are available for inspection. If the old test certificate has only a few months to run, get a new one if you can do so without too much expense - it will make the car much more saleable. You're likely to sell your car more quickly and get a better price if you sell at the right time of year. It's always best to sell in the spring or summer rather than in the winter.

BUYING NEW

This is the most expensive option, but also the most secure – you are protected against anything going wrong with the car.

Find your dealer

Look in Yellow Pages to identify the local dealers who sell the make of car you want. If there's more than one, it's well worth contacting all of them – just because they sell the same cars, it doesn't mean that they will offer you the same deal!

What's included?

When you've driven the car, and decided on the specification and colour that suits you, check on what will be included in the price (are number plates, road tax and delivery charges included?). Most new cars are sold with a comprehensive warranty package, which will often include breakdown insurance.

Start haggling!

Unless you're buying a particularly sought-after model, the manufacturer's list price is the absolute maximum which you should pay, and there's always scope for the dealer to offer a discount. You'll almost certainly get a better deal at a time of year when the dealer isn't selling many cars, for instance around Christmas.

BUYING SECOND-HAND

The safest way is to buy from a recognised dealer. Riskier alternatives are to buy at auction (not recommended for the average buyer) or privately. If you can't afford to have the car inspected professionally, take a knowledgeable friend with you, and bear in mind the following points.

• Don't buy the first car to catch your attention. If you've never driven the model of car you're thinking of buying, it's a good idea to view and drive several examples so that you can compare them.

• If you're buying privately, ask to see the service receipts and test certificates. This will help to establish that the car hasn't been stolen, and that the recorded mileage is genuine. Always ask to view the car at the seller's private address, to make sure that it isn't being sold by an unscrupulous dealer posing as a private seller.

• Don't be put off by high mileage. Most modern cars are capable of completing 100,000 miles or more without major problems, provided that they have been well-maintained. A high mileage car which has been used mainly for motorway cruising may be in better shape than a low-mileage car which has been used for short journeys.

• Check the service history. The service book supplied with the car when new should have been completed and stamped by an authorised garage after each service. Cars with a full service history ("fsh") usually command a higher price than those without. If the car is 3 years old or more, check that it has a new or very recent MoT certificate.

Second-hand woes
Many dealers offer comprehensive warranties, but beware of some of the warranty plans sold with second-hand cars. You'll often find that there's a maximum claim limit, which may be so low that it limits the warranty to very minor problems. Items such as clutch and brake linings, drivebelts and cooling system hoses - the components most likely to cause problems on an older car - will almost certainly be excluded. If it's suggested that you pay extra for a warranty, read the small print carefully – you'll probably find that it's not worth the extra.

BUYING AND SELLING A CAR

• Don't view in the dark or wet. Water on the bodywork can give a misleading impression of the condition of the paintwork.

• Check the indicated mileage, and ask yourself if it's genuine. If the car has covered a high mileage, there will often be signs of wear on the driver's seat, in the driver's footwell around the pedals and on the pedal rubbers.

• Check for rust, and for signs of new or mis-matched paint, which might show that the car has been involved in an accident. Check the tyres for signs of unusual wear or damage, and check that the car "sits" evenly on its suspension, with all four corners at the same height.

• Open the bonnet. Check for any obvious fluid leakage (oil, water, brake fluid), then start the engine and listen for any unusual noises. Also check for signs of excessive exhaust smoke. Blue smoke often indicates worn engine components, which may prove expensive to repair.

• Check the locks. One key should operate all the locks and the ignition switch – if not, it's likely that the car has been broken into at some stage, and one or more of the locks has been replaced.

• Drive the car, and test the brakes, steering and gearbox. Make sure that the car doesn't pull to one side, and check that the steering feels positive and that the gears can be selected satisfactorily. Listen for any unusual noises or vibration, and keep an eye on the instruments and warning lights to make sure that they're working.

• Don't be rushed into a deal. There are plenty more cars to look at.

Check this out!
There are several organisations which, for a small fee, will carry out checks on a car to ensure that there's no outstanding finance owed by a previous owner, and that the car has not been declared an insurance write-off. If money is owed to a finance company, the car could be repossessed, and you may have no right to compensation! The same applies if you inadvertently buy a stolen car.

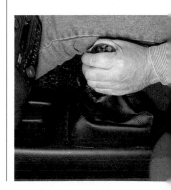

CONVERSION
FACTORS

Length (distance)

Inches (in)	x 25.4	Millimetres (mm)	x 0.0394	Inches (in)	
Inches (in)	x 2.54	Centimetres (cm)	x 0.394	Inches (in)	
Feet (ft)	x 0.305	Metres (m)	x 3.281	Feet (ft)	
Miles	x 1.609	Kilometres (km)	x 0.621	Miles	

Volume (capacity)

Cubic inches (cu in; cm^3)	x 16.387	Cubic centimetres (cc; cm^3)	x 0.061	Cubic inches (cu in; cm^3)
Pints (pt)	x 0.568	Litres (l)	x 1.76	Pints (pt)
Gallons (gal)	x 4.546	Litres (l)	x 0.22	Gallons (gal)

Mass (weight)

Ounces (oz)	x 28.35	Grams (g)	x 0.035	Ounces (oz)
Pounds (lb)	x 0.454	Kilograms (kg)	x 2.205	Pounds (lb)

Pressure

Pounds-force per square inch (psi; lbf/in^2; lb/in^2)	x 0.070	Kilograms-force per square centimetre (kgf/cm^2; kg/cm^2)	x 14.223	Pounds-force per square inch (psi; lbf/in^2; lb/in^2)
Pounds-force per square inch (psi; lbf/in^2; lb/in^2)	x 0.069	Bars	x 14.5	Pounds-force per square inch (psi; lbf/in^2; lb/in^2)

CONVERSION FACTORS

Power

Horsepower (hp; bhp)	x 0.746	Kilowatts (kW)	x 1.34	Horsepower (hp; bhp)
Horsepower (hp; bhp)	x 1.014	Metric horsepower (PS)	x 0.986	Horsepower (hp; bhp)

Velocity (speed)

Miles per hour (mph)	x 1.609	Kilometres per hour (kph; km/h)	x 0.621	Miles per hour (mph)

Temperature

Degrees Fahrenheit $= (°C \times 1.8) + 32$

Degrees Celsius $= (°F - 32) \times 0.56$

Fuel consumption

Miles per gallon (mpg)	x 0.354	Kilometres per litre (km/l)	x 2.825	Miles per gallon (mpg)

Note: The usual measure for fuel consumption in Europe is litres per 100 kilometres (l/100 km); there are no simple conversion factors for this – both 'miles per gallon' and 'litres per 100 kilometres' have to be divided into 282 to convert to the other, eg:

30 mpg: $\dfrac{282}{30}$ = 9.4 l/100 km

9.4 l/100 km: $\dfrac{282}{9.4}$ = 30 mpg

Miles per gallon (mpg)	x 0.22	Miles per litre (mpl; m/l)	x 4.546	Miles per gallon (mpg)

ACCIDENT
REPORT FORM

Use these pages to record all the relevant details in the event of an accident. You should transfer all the information recorded on this page onto the Motor Vehicle Accident Report form which you can obtain from your insurance company.

Other vehicle details

Driver

Full name ....

Address ....

    ....

    ....

Telephone number ....

Learner? ....

Owner (if different)

Full name ....

Address ....

    ....

    ....

Telephone number ....

Vehicle

Make..

Model ....

Registration number ....

Insurance

Company ....

Type of cover ....

Policy number (if known)..

ACCIDENT REPORT FORM

Circumstances of accident

General
Date ....
Time ....
Place...
Weather conditions ....
Approximate speed ....
Were the police called? ....
Details of station/officers attending ....
Did anyone sustain injury?...

Witnesses
1 Full name ....
Address ....
....
....
Telephone number ....

2 Full name ....
Address ....
....
....
Telephone number ....

What happened?
Record all details of the incident. Include:

- The state of the road
- Whether all people involved were wearing seat belts
- If the accident was at night, were the streetlights on and were all vehicles' lights working?

Make a rough sketch, including:

- The width and layout of the road, and its approaches
- The directions and identities of all vehicles
- Relative vehicle positions at time of impact
- Road signs and road markings
- Names of streets and roads
- The location of any marks on the road and debris

Take photos, if you can

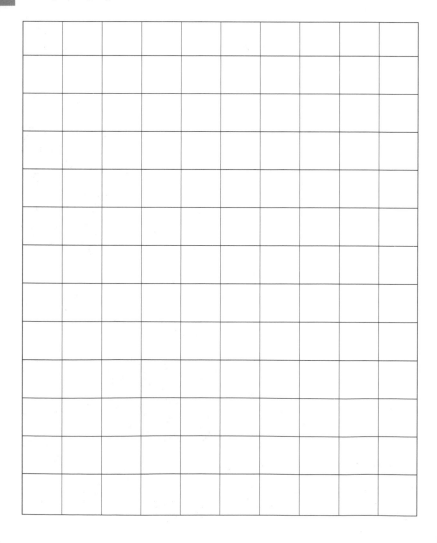

GLOSSARY

The following information isn't intended to be an Automotive waffle-to-English dictionary, but it should help you to understand some of the more common terms which you'll come across when discussing your car with your local garage, or when talking to the local pub-bore!

ABS – Anti-lock Braking System. Uses sensors at each wheel to sense when the wheels are about to lock, and releases the brakes to prevent locking.

Air bag – An inflatable bag which inflates in the event of a head-on collision to protect the driver and/or front passenger from injury. Driver's air bags are usually mounted in the steering wheel and passenger's airbags are usually mounted in the dashboard.

Air conditioning – A system which enables the temperature of the air inside the car to be lowered, and dehumidifies the air. This allows more comfort and rapid demisting.

Air filter – A renewable paper or foam filter which removes foreign particles from the air which is sucked into the engine.

Alternator – An electrical generator which is driven by the engine. Its job is to provide electricity for the car's electrical system when the engine's running, and to charge the battery.

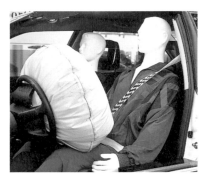

Antifreeze – A fluid which is added to water to produce coolant. The antifreeze stops the coolant freezing in cold weather, and prevents corrosion inside the engine.

Battery – A "reservoir" which stores electricity. Provides the power to start the engine, and power for the electrical systems when the engine's stopped, and is charged by the alternator when the engine's running.

Brake fluid – A hydraulic fluid resistant to high temperatures, used in hydraulic braking systems, and some hydraulic clutch systems.

Brake pad – A metal plate, with a pad of hard-wearing friction material bonded to one side. When the brakes are applied, the hydraulic pistons in the brake caliper push the pads against the brake disc.

Brake shoe – A curved metal former with friction material bonded to the outside surface. When the brake are applied, the hydraulic pistons in the wheel cylinder push the brake shoes against the brake drum.

Cam belt – See Timing belt.

Carburettor – A device which is used to mix air and petrol in the correct proportions required for burning by the engine. Superseded on modern cars by fuel injection systems.

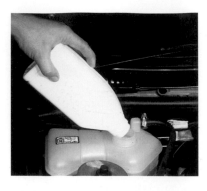

Catalytic converter – A device built fitted in the exhaust system which reduces the amount of harmful gases released into the atmosphere.

Choke – Either the device which reduces the amount of air entering a carburettor during cold starting (in order to provide extra petrol), or a term to describe the passage where the throttle valve is located in a carburettor.

Clutch – A friction device which allows two rotating components to be coupled together smoothly, without the need for either rotating component to stop moving.

Coolant – A liquid consisting of a mixture of water and antifreeze, used in a car's engine cooling system.

GLOSSARY

Coolant sensor – A sensor used in an engine management system, or possibly in several other systems to provide information on the temperature of the engine coolant.

Cubic capacity – The total volume inside an engine which is swept by the movement of all the pistons.

Depreciation – The reduction in value of a car as time passes.

Derv – Abbreviation for Diesel-Engines Road Vehicle. A term often used for diesel fuel.

Diagnostic light – A warning light on the instrument panel which illuminates when a fault code has been stored in an electronic control unit memory.

Diesel engine – An engine which relies on the heat produced when compressing air to ignite the fuel, and so doesn't need an ignition system. Diesel engines have a much higher compression ratio than petrol engines.

Dipstick – A metal or plastic rod with graduated marks used to check the level of a fluid.

Distributor – A device used to distribute the ignition HT circuit current to the individual spark plugs. The distributor may also control the ignition timing.

Distributor cap – A plastic cap which fits on top of the distributor. The cap contains electrodes (one for each cylinder) inside which the rotor arm rotates to distribute the HT circuit current to the correct spark plug.

DOHC – Double OverHead Camshafts. An engine with two camshafts, where one operates the inlet valves, and the other operates the exhaust valves. Allows the valves to be positioned for greater efficiency (improved flow of mixture and exhaust gases).

Drivebelt – A belt, usually made from rubber, used to transmit drive between two pulleys or sprockets. Often used to drive the camshafts (see Timing belt), and engine ancillaries.

Driveshaft – Term used to describe a shaft which transmits drive from a differential to one wheel.

Excess – The part of an insurance claim paid by the insured.

Expansion tank – A container used in many car's cooling systems to collect the overflow from the cooling system as the coolant heats up and expands.

Fan – Electric or engine-driven fan mounted at the front of the engine compartment and designed to cool the radiator.

Fan belt – another term for a drivebelt. The name arose because on older cars a drivebelt was used to drive the cooling fan. Electric cooling fans are used on most modern cars.

Firing order – The order in which the pistons in the cylinders of an engine reach their firing points.

Four-stroke – A term used to describe the four operating strokes of a piston in a car engine.

FSH – Full Service History. A written record which shows that a car has been serviced from new in accordance with the manufacturer's recommendations.

Fuel filter – A renewable filter which removes foreign particles from the fuel.

Fuel injection – A method of injecting a measured amount of fuel into an engine. Used on all diesel engines, and used on most modern petrol engines in place of a carburettor.

Fuel pump – A device which pumps fuel from the fuel tank to the fuel system.

GLOSSARY

Gearbox – A group of gears and shafts in a housing positioned between the engine and differential, used to keep a car's engine within its safe operating speed range as the speed of the car changes.

Glow plug – An electrical heating device fitted to a diesel engine to help the engine to start from cold, and to reduce the smoke produced immediately after start-up. Each cylinder usually has its own glow plug.

Heater matrix – A small radiator mounted in the engine's coolant circuit which provides hot air for the car's heating system. Hot coolant flows through the matrix, which heats the surrounding air.

Horsepower – A measurement of the power of an engine. Brake horsepower (BHP) is a measure of the power available to stop a moving body.

Idle speed – The running speed of an engine when the throttle is closed.

Ignition system – The electrical system which provides the spark to ignite the air/fuel mixture in a petrol engine.

Inertia reel – Automatic type of seat belt mechanism which allows the wearer to move freely in normal use, but locks when the car decelerates suddenly or the wearer moves suddenly.

Jump leads – Heavy electrical cables fitted with clamps to enable a car's battery to be connected to another for emergency starting.

Kickdown – A device used on an automatic transmission which allows a lower gear to be selected for improved acceleration by fully depressing the accelerator pedal.

Knocking (Pinking) – A metallic noise from the engine often caused by the ignition timing being incorrect or a build-up of carbon inside the engine. The noise is due to pressure waves which cause the cylinder walls to vibrate.

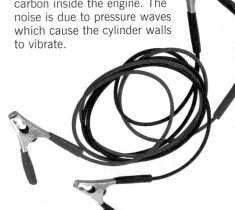

Laminated windscreen – A windscreen which has a thin plastic layer sandwiched between two layers of toughened glass. It will not shatter or craze when hit.

Leaded petrol – 4-star petrol. Has a low amount of lead added during manufacture in addition to the natural lead found in crude oil.

Lead Replacement Petrol (LRP) – A leaded petrol (4-star) equivalent with no lead added.

LHM – A special type of mineral-based hydraulic fluid used in Citroën hydraulic systems.

LPG – Liquefied Petroleum Gas. A mixture of liquefied petroleum gases, such as propane and butane, which are obtained from crude oil. Used in some engines as an alternative to petrol and diesel fuel.

Multi-point fuel injection – A fuel injection system which has one fuel injector for each cylinder of the engine.

Multi-valve – An engine with more than two valves per cylinder. Usually four valves per cylinder (2 inlet and 2 exhaust valves), or sometimes three valves per cylinder (2 inlet valves and 1 exhaust valve).

OHC – OverHead Camshaft. An engine layout where the camshaft is mounted above the valves. Because the camshaft operates the valves directly (via the valve gear), an OHC engine is more efficient than an OHV engine.

OHV – OverHead Valve. An engine layout where the valves are located in the cylinder head, but the valve gear is operated by pushrods from a camshaft located lower in the cylinder block.

Oil cooler – A small radiator fitted in the engine oil circuit, positioned in a cooling airflow to cool the oil. Often used on diesel engines and high-performance petrol engines.

Oil filter – A renewable filter which removes foreign particles from the engine oil.

PAS – See Power assisted steering.

Pinking – See Knocking.

GLOSSARY

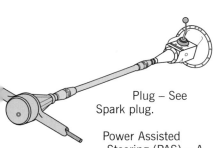

Plug – See Spark plug.

Power Assisted Steering (PAS) – A system which uses hydraulic pressure to provide assistance when the driver turns the steering wheel.

Pre-ignition – See Knocking.

Propeller shaft – The shaft which transmits drive from the manual gearbox or automatic transmission to the differential in a front-engined, rear-wheel-drive or four-wheel-drive car.

Radiator – A cooling device, located in a cooling airflow, through which a hot liquid is passed. A radiator is made up of fine tubes and fins to allow rapid cooling of the liquid inside.

Refrigerant – The substance used to absorb heat in an air conditioning system. The refrigerant is changed from a gas to a liquid and *vice versa* during the air conditioning process.

Rotary (Wankel) engine – An engine which has a triangular shaped rotor instead of the pistons used in a conventional engine. The rotor rotates in a housing shaped like a broad figure-of-eight. Very few cars have this type of engine.

Rotor arm – A rotating arm in a distributor, which distributes the HT circuit voltage to correct spark plug. An electrode on the rotor arm distributes the voltage to electrodes in the distributor cap, which are connected to the HT leads.

Running-on – A tendency for the engine to keep on running after the ignition has been switched off. Often caused by incorrect ignition timing, the wrong grade of fuel, or a poorly maintained engine.

Screenwash – See Washer fluid.

Servo – A device for increasing the normal effort applied to a control.

Shock absorber – A device used to damp out the up-and-down movement of the suspension when the car hits a bump in the road.

Single-point fuel injection – A fuel injection system which has a single fuel injector.

SOHC – Single OverHead Camshaft. An OHC engine with a single camshaft.

Spark plug – A device which provides the spark in a petrol engine's combustion chamber in order to ignite the air/fuel mixture. The HT circuit voltage jumps between two electrodes on the spark plug, creating a spark.

Starter motor – An electric motor used to start the engine. A pinion gear on the starter motor engages with a large gear on the engine's flywheel, which turns the crankshaft.

Sump – The main reservoir for the engine oil.

Supercharger – A device which uses an engine-driven turbine (usually driven from the crankshaft) to drive a compressor which forces air into the engine. This provides better air/fuel mixture flow into the engine and therefore more power.

Suspension – A general term used to describe the system which insulates a car's body from the roadwheels, and keeps all four roadwheels in contact with the road surface.

Tachometer (rev. counter) – Indicates engine speed in revolutions per minute.

Thermostat – A device which aids engine warm-up by preventing the coolant from flowing through the radiator, until a pre-determined temperature is reached. The thermostat then regulates the temperature of the coolant.

Timing belt (cam belt) – Fabric or rubber toothed drivebelt, used to transmit drive from the crankshaft to the camshaft(s).

Timing chain – Metal flexible link chain which engages with sprockets, used to transmit drive from the crankshaft to the camshaft(s).

Toe-in/toe-out – The angle at which the front wheels point inwards or outwards from the straight-ahead position when the steering is positioned straight-ahead. Toe-in is when the front edges of the wheels point inwards.

Torque wrench – A tool used to tighten fasteners to a prescribed tightness.

Toughened windscreen – A windscreen which when hit will shatter in a particular way to produce blunt-edged fragments, or will craze but remain intact.

Transmission – A general term used to describe some or all of the drivetrain components excluding the engine. Commonly used to describe automatic gearboxes.

GLOSSARY

Turbocharger – A device which uses a turbine driven by the engine exhaust gases to drive a compressor which forces air into the engine. This provides better air/fuel mixture flow into the engine and therefore more power.

Twin-cam – Abbreviation for twin overhead camshafts – see DOHC.

Unleaded petrol – Petrol which had no lead added during manufacture, but still has the natural lead content of crude oil.

Valves – A device which opens of closes to stop or allow gas or fluid flow.

Valve clearance – The clearance between the top of a valve and the camshaft, necessary to allow the valve to close fully, and to allow for expansion of the valvegear components. Often adjusted by adjusting the clearance between the tappet and camshaft.

16-valve – A term used to describe a four-cylinder engine with four valves per cylinder, usually two exhaust and two inlet valves. Gives improved efficiency due to improved air/fuel mixture and exhaust gas flow in the combustion chambers.

Voluntary excess – see Excess.

Wankel engine – See Rotary engine.

Washer fluid – The water used to wash the windscreen, etc. Often with a detergent additive to improve cleaning and resist freezing.

Washer jet – The nozzle which directs washer fluid onto the windscreen.

Wheel alignment – The process of checking the toe-in/toe-out, and sometimes the camber and castor angles of the wheels. On most cars, only the toe-in/toe-out can be adjusted. Incorrect wheel alignment can cause tyre wear and poor handling.

Wheel balancing – The process of adding small weights to the rim of a wheel so that there are no out-of-balance forces when the wheel rotates.

Wheel brace – The tool used to slacken the nuts or bolts holding the wheel on the car.

DISTANCE
CHART

DISTANCES BETWEEN EUROPEAN CITIES

Note: Distances are given in kilometres

Amsterdam																			
1341	Belfast																		
669	1906	Berlin																	
204	1150	781	Brussels																
738	2033	384	890	Copenhagen															
1053	165	1618	862	1745	Dublin														
1289	251	1855	1098	1982	416	Edinburgh													
885	1492	1121	703	1367	1204	1441	Geneva												
1204	2441	505	1316	795	2153	2390	1656	Helsinki											
2665	3703	2413	2621	2767	3415	3652	2275	2389	Istanbul										
1637	2874	938	1749	1228	2586	2823	2089	433	2041	Leningrad*									
2322	2653	2888	2127	3015	2365	2601	2000	3423	4149	3856	Lisbon								
719	722	1284	528	1411	434	612	870	1819	3081	2252	2031	London							
391	1338	767	218	915	1050	1286	486	1302	2466	1735	2188	716	Luxembourg						
1812	2143	2378	1617	2505	1855	2091	1440	2913	3589	3346	658	1521	1678	Madrid					
1321	2616	967	1473	583	2328	2565	1950	690	3350	1123	3598	1994	1498	3088	Oslo				
504	965	1069	308	1196	677	914	538	1604	2741	2037	1820	343	376	1310	1779	Paris			
950	1999	350	906	760	1711	1948	979	859	1983	1292	2850	1377	733	2340	1343	1037	Prague		
1665	2372	1505	1471	1859	2084	2320	885	2040	2218	2473	2579	1750	1254	2019	2442	1417	2505	Rome	
1368	2663	1014	1520	630	2375	2612	1997	165	3397	598	3645	2041	1545	3135	525	1826	1390	2489	S

*St Peterburg

RADIO
FREQUENCIES

BBC NATIONAL RADIO

Radio station	1	2	3	4	5
Aberdeen	98.3	88.7	90.9	95.3	693
Aberystwyth	98.3	88.7	90.9	104.0	990
Anglesey					693
Ayr	99.1	89.5	91.7	104.3	909
Barnstaple					909
Belfast	99.7	90.1	92.3	96.0	909
Berwick-upon-Tweed	99.7	90.1	92.3	94.5	693
Birmingham	97.9	88.3	90.5	92.7	693
Blackpool	98.2	88.6	90.8	93.0	909
Bournemouth	98.2	88.5	90.7	92.9	693
Brighton	98.8	89.1	91.3	93.5	693
Bristol	99.5	89.9	92.1	94.3	909
Burghead				198	
Cambridge	99.7	90.1	92.3	94.5	
Campbeltown					909
Cardiff	99.5	89.9	92.1	94.3	909
Carlisle	97.7	88.1	90.3	92.5/1485	693
Channel Islands	97.1	89.6	91.1	94.8	693
Chelmsford					909
Colwyn Bay					909
Darlington	98.1	88.5	90.7	92.9	
Derby					693
Douglas	98.0	88.4	90.6	92.8	
Dover	99.1	90.0	92.4	94.4	909
Droitwich				198	
Dundee	97.9	88.3	90.5	94.9	909
Edinburgh	99.5	89.9	92.1	95.8	909
Enniskillen				774	
Exeter					909
Folkstone					909
Fort William	99.2	89.3	91.5	95.9	693
Glasgow	99.5	89.9	92.1	95.8	909
Gloucester					693
Guildford	97.7	88.1	90.3	92.5	
Hastings					693
Holyhead	99.4	89.8	92.0	103.6	

BBC Radio	1	2	3	4	5
Hull	98.3	88.8	90.9	93.1	909
Inverness	99.2	89.6	91.8	103.6	693
Ipswich	99.3	89.7	91.9	94.1	909
Isle of Man					693
Isle of Wight					693
Leeds	98.9	89.3	91.5	93.7	909
Lincoln	98.9	89.3	91.5	93.7	
Liverpool	98.9	89.3	91.5	93.7	909
London	98.5	88.8	91.0	93.2/720	909
Londonderry	98.3	88.7	90.9	94.9/720	909
Luton	98.2	88.6	90.8	93.0	
Maidstone					909
Manchester	98.9	89.3	91.5	93.7	909
Middlesborough					693
Milford Haven	98.9	89.3	91.5	104.9	
Newbury	99.1	89.5	91.7	93.9	
Newcastle-upon-Tyne	98.1	88.5	90.7	92.9/603	693
Newquay	99.3	89.7	91.9	94.1	
Northampton					693
Norwich	99.3	89.7	91.9	94.1	693
Nottingham					693
Orkney Islands	98.9	89.3	91.5	95.9	693
Oxford	99.1	89.5	91.7	93.9	693
Pembroke					693
Peterborough	99.7	90.1	92.3	94.5	
Plymouth	97.7	88.1	90.3	92.5/774	693
Portsmouth					909
Redmoss				1449	
Redruth				756	
Salisbury					693
Scarborough	98.9	89.3	91.5	93.7	909
Sheffield	98.9	89.3	91.5	93.7	909
Shetland Islands	97.9	88.3	90.5	94.9	693
Shrewsbury	97.9	88.3	90.5	92.7	
Southampton	98.2	88.5	90.7	92.9	
Southend					909
Stoke					693
Stranraer					909
Swansea					909
Taunton	99.5	89.9	92.1	94.3	
Thurso	99.7	90.1	92.3	104.5	
Torquay					693
Westerglen				198	
Weymouth					693
Wick					693
Worcester	98.2	88.3	90.5	92.7	
Workington					909
Wrexham	88.9	91.1	91.1	98.5	
York					909

RADIO FREQUENCIES

INDEPENDENT NATIONAL RADIO

CLASSIC FM RADIO

Aberdeen	100.5
Aberystwyth	101.1
Belfast	101.9
Birmingham	100.1
Blackpool	101.8
Brighton	100.9
Bristol	101.7
Cardiff	101.7
Carlisle	99.9
Douglas	100.2
Dundee	100.1
Edinburgh	101.7
Exeter	100.0
Glasgow	101.7
Guernsey	101.3
Hannington	100.3
Haverfordwest	100.5
Hull	100.5
Inverness	101.4
Jersey	101.3
Leeds	101.1
Liverpool	101.1
London	100.9
Londonderry	100.5
Manchester	101.1
Milton Keynes	100.4
Newcastle-upon-Tyne	100.3
Norwich	101.5
Oxford	101.3
Perth	101.7
Peterborough	101.9
Plymouth	100.0
Redruth	101.5
Sheffield	101.1
Southampton	100.3
St Davids	100.5
The Borders	100.9

TALK RADIO UK MW

Boston	1107
Bournemouth	1053
Brighton	1053
Brookmans Park	1089
Clipstone	1071
Dartford Tunnel	1089
Droitwich	1053
Dumfries	1053
Dundee	1053
Exeter	1053
Fareham	1107
Gatwick	1107
Hull	1053
Lisnagarvey	1089
Londonderry	1053
Lydd	1107
Moorside Edge	1089
Newcastle	1071
Plymouth	1053
Postwick	1053
Redmoss	1089
Redruth	1089
Rosemarkie	1053
Stockton	1053
Tonbridge	1053
Torbay	1107
Wallasey	1107
Washford	1089
Westerglen	1089

VIRGIN RADIO MW

Bournemouth	1197	Newcastle	1215
Brighton	1197	Oxford	1197
Brookmans Park	1215	Plymouth	1215
Cambridge	1197	Postwick	1215
Dartford Tunnel	1197	Reading	1233
Dundee	1242	Redmoss	1215
Fareham	1215	Sheffield	1233
Gloucester	1197	Sideway	1242
Guildford	1260	Stockton	1242
Hoo	1197	Swindon	1233
Hull	1215	Torbay	1197
Kings Heath	1233	Trowell	1197
Lisnagarvey	1215	Wallasey	1197
Lydd	1260	Washford	1215
Manningtree	1233	Westerglen	1215
Moorside Edge	1215		

INDEX

INDEX

T

V

W